PERS⊙NAL VILLAGE ™

HOW TO HAVE PEOPLE IN YOUR LIFE BY CHOICE, NOT CHANCE

D0964120

Marvin Thomas, MSW

The names of individuals and identifying details cited in this book have been changed to protect their privacy.

Published by
Milestone Books
P.O. Box 19732
Seattle, WA 98109

Library of congress Cataloging in Publication Data
Thomas, Marvin
    Personal village : how to have people in your life by choice, not chance /Marvin Thomas. -- 1st ed. -- Seattle, Wash. : Hara Publishing, 2004.

    p. ; cm.
    "Milestone Books."
    ISBN: 1-887542-08-6

    1. Interpersonal relations. 2. Interpersonal communication. 3. Social interaction. I. Title.

HM1106 .T56 2003   2003109653
153.6--dc22   0310

Printed in the United States of America
10   9   8   7   6   5   4   3   2

Cover design by Iskra Johnson
Book design by Tami Taylor

This book is dedicated to
Swami Chidvilasananda

per•son•al vil•lage, /prs ( )nel /'vil /ij
1: The net of people surrounding each individual—close family members, friends, fellow
students, teachers, co-workers, bosses, neighbors, the doctor, the mechanic, and the grocery
store clerk. It includes everyone an individual
knows and all familiar strangers. **2**: The most
immediate dimension of community for each
individual. **3**: The foundation of society's complex network of overlapping interactions. **4**: A
concept first introduced in the 1930s by Jacob
Moreno when he introduced the phrase *social
atom* to describe a constellation of people that
form the atomic level of community for each
individual. **5**: The group of people that social
psychologists describe using the terms *personal
network* and *convoy*.

CONTENTS

A Word From The Author

I am a man on a mission. My mission is to revitalize community for myself and everyone I can reach.

Half a lifetime ago, in my work as a psychotherapist, I realized that many of the people who came to see me would not have been in my office if they had experienced and were still embedded in a strong, supportive circle of people. As a young father and professional, I began to recognize that this rich circle was missing in my own life as well. At the same time, I began to realize that some people seemed to have a knack for surrounding themselves with people and creating intimacy, abilities I lacked.

I also shared the growing sense of distress that many feel about what our modern world is doing to our humanity. It was obvious that our sense of community was being seriously eroded in our headlong race into a future of modern wonders. I have watched from my comfortable place in the Western world as we've lived through the greatest technological leap forward the human race had ever taken: a leap both exciting and promising, like nothing before in history, but with a price.

I grew up in a traditional, strong extended family that had just migrated into the city from the farm culture upon which America was built. My family shared the farm values of hard work and of community. Babies were born at home and the old folks died in each other's arms. Life was hard, but regardless of what happened a strong circle of community always supported everyone. Even though I had not learned the skills necessary to create such a community for myself, I saw firsthand the power it could hold in leading a rich life.

As a young man, just launched into a career in the space program, I found myself suddenly caught up in technical, hurry-hurry, modern America. It was not long before I recognized that something was missing. I had to find a way to balance this new exciting world with the strong sense of community in which I had grown up.

This need started as confusion as I experienced the collision between our humanity and the pressures of modern life. Then it turned into alarm as I became aware of current problems in the context of the history I was studying. Most of the people I talked with saw the same problems, but they tended to respond either by ignoring them or by complaining. I decided I was going to apply what I knew from my community-based childhood to improve the quality of life for myself, my family, and the people around me. I realized that to do less would simply be adding to the problems that worried me. Eventually I left my career as an engineer and studied to become a social worker.

My growing awareness of the necessity for vital communities led to what has become a burning passion over the last thirty years. It was urgent that I find a way to think about personal communities and develop a way to strengthen them. I closely studied the communal dimensions in my work as an organizational consultant and psychotherapist, and I explored the back alleys of our culture at every level, watching people on the streets, in malls, in classrooms, in business settings, in the halls of government. I studied anthropology, sociology, the world's religions, and depth psychology. I poured over all the literature written about community and immersed myself in both current affairs and history.

My efforts eventually gave me a way to think about personal community and allowed me to develop a body of material that anyone can use to create a supportive cast for themselves. Before I could write about the topic of personal community, my earlier engineering training impelled me to develop a theory about all community systems, from the most immediate to those of every level of society and even to the entire global community. What started out as a single book about personal community has turned into a series of books that I am driven to write. I identify with George Bernard Shaw when he said: *"I want to be thoroughly used up when I die. The harder I work, the more I live. Life is no brief candle to me. It is a splendid torch which I want to make burn as brightly as I can before I pass it on to following generations."*

What I learned taught me how to surround myself with a strong circle of people. The professionals called this immediate circle a *personal network* or *convoy*. I came to call it my *personal village*. The first in my series of books is about how to create community at the most immediate, personal level. You are holding that book in your hand.

What I will describe in this book is not a one-time effort. Just like caring for your health or finances or career, your personal village will require continual attention and tending. Community is not a simple process like throwing a party or changing the tires on a car. It is not a step-by-step process like baking cookies. It does not have a beginning or an end. Like the quest to know God, community can be embraced in many ways and approached from many directions simultaneously. I have tried in this book to show you many of the levels on which you can enhance your own circle of important people. This book will not cover everything you need to know, but it will get you started. It will change your life for the better and improve the lives of those around you.

Enjoy *Personal Village*. You now have a roadmap to creating and revitalizing your own personal community.

> *May you blossom fully. May your loved ones blossom fully, and may everyone living on Mother Earth blossom fully to the ultimate that is our human heritage. May every person come into perfect harmony with their highest self and with each other.*

HOW TO USE THIS BOOK

A book about community is like a cookbook. Community is at the very core of what it is to be human, so it is not like talking about a nice tidy logical flow from A to B, as you would find in a math book. Rather, it is more like talking about how to cook a stew: there are certain general principles that the cook applies, and then the artistic expression of the cook finds its way to a luscious result. Although it is impossible to describe community as if it were a sequential process, it is necessary when writing a book to follow some logical flow. I chose to organize this book from the least intimate to the most intimate. It may appear from that organization that intimacy comes last, but in reality we first enter community as an infant where intimacy is highest. Our experience of community happens on many levels at once. What I have tried to do in this book is describe the different dimensions of those levels. You will become the cook and apply what fits for you at the moment. Your community will be in a constant state of flux. The more recipes you have at your finger tips, the better you will be able to create what you need, and the better you will be at surrounding yourself with the right people at any given period in your life.

This book is purposely written to give you many ways to get the ideas. The first two chapters offer an understanding of community as it stands in today's world and define the personal village concept in a strong historical context. Chapter Three is a discussion about intimacy and lays the foundation for the ideas to follow. But if you want to start right in on the practical how-to-do-it instructions of creating or strengthening your personal village, skip directly to Chapter Four.

For those who like to scan, a brief abstract at the beginning of each chapter provides an overview of what's to come. At the end of each chapter, you will find summaries of the major ideas, and throughout the text are sidebars that highlight the central ideas.

This book carefully lays out the major issues you will need to know about if you want your personal village to thrive. Most chapters are relatively short—about one bus ride or lunch break long. You can grasp each concept easily in a short time. This book is organized so that you can read it from cover to cover, or you can open it at random and, in short order, what you are reading will make sense.

At the end of each chapter, I have included a list of other resources you might find useful for expanding your understanding of community. You will also find a few films on the list. The visual dimension of film will bring into focus the reality that community is complex, rich, often painful, challenging, and ultimately very human in ways too difficult to capture in a how-to book.

At the very end of the book you will find the Community Effectiveness Test (page 252) you can use to evaluate any part of your community system. The Personal Village Discussion Guide (page 254) contains a series of questions you can use to begin a conversation about the ideas that are contained in this book.

So mark it up. Make notes. Fold the pages. Stuff it full of articles. Spill coffee on it. Share it with others in your life. Make it your own. When you are finished, toss it in the corner like an old rag doll. When you need ideas about how to deal with changes in your life or to re-people your personal village, it will be waiting.

ENJOY!

INTRODUCTION

Community is the ever-present foundation supporting close to three million years of human evolution. Our ancient ancestors were more apelike than human, yet there is much evidence that they lived a communal life. They cooperated in scaring off the predators waiting to eat them. They supported the mothers who were caring for babies. They gathered food collectively, and the children depended upon their elders to teach them how to live off the land. Our interdependence went on for so long that community eventually became a part of our genetic heritage.

When we see the great lengths to which people will go for each other, this genetic loading toward community becomes very evident. It is so embedded in our DNA to help one another that under extreme situations we are even willing to sacrifice our lives. When the Russian nuclear reactor blew up at Chernobyl, it was believed that the core of the reactor would melt into the ground, with dire consequences. A plan was developed to dig a tunnel under the reactor and to divert an entire river beneath the core as a way to cool it. Men eagerly came forward to work around the clock to dig the tunnel, knowing full well that they would die from the radiation. They succeeded with the tunnel, and they all died. They willingly made this sacrifice for their families and countrymen.

All great scientific, economic, and political advances have stood on the shoulders of well-integrated communities. We are the only species on the planet that crafts complex art, tools, and toys as evidence of our passing. Thousands of years ago our ancestors crawled into caves and drew the magnificent pictures on the walls that are still visible today. We have developed highly symbolic languages, created music, and danced with abstract ideas like mathematics and the question of why we exist. We have enormous abilities, and we have used our large brains to devise ways to magnify those abilities in the most amazing ways.

For eons, finding food consumed the efforts of almost everyone. When food was plentiful we spent our spare time exploring, playing, and telling stories. But often food was scarce, and famine and starvation were a frequent part of living a hunter-gatherer life. Gradually, we collectively learned how to assure a more reliable supply of food by keeping herds and growing crops. By amplifying our ability to have a steady supply of food, we were able to settle down in one place. The guarantee of food freed up a few people to follow other activities, like pottery, tool making, and the development of formal spiritual systems. This was the beginning of small settlements that eventually evolved into towns and finally civilizations.

Not long after we solved the food problem, we discovered ways to magnify our physical abilities, first through levers and wheels and today with huge machines, like airplanes. As with food production, the sophistication with which we have amplified our physical strength is still growing, even today.

Settling down in one place with an assured food source allowed written language to develop. Our ability to exchange information increased from the crude drawings of long ago to written language. Methods of communication have now evolved to include the digital transmissions and satellites that allow us to communicate around the globe instantly. As a result of this evolution, our ability to communicate has multiplied over and over.

More recently, the critical mass of people, ideas, and technology has boosted our ability to create more complex systems. Computers do for our minds what levers do for our muscles. The resulting benefits to humanity have been staggering. We have only begun to see the advantages that computers will bring to our ability to amplify our minds.

Magnifying our abilities has only been possible in the cooperative environment that exists within community, where shared resources encourage creativity and innovation. Yet despite its importance, few of us give the idea of community more than a passing thought. We hardly notice it when it works, yet we would cease to exist if it disappeared. This may seem dramatic, but imagine your life in complete isolation with no human contact.

The scientific research is very clear; we are more vulnerable to an entire host of physical and emotional difficulties if our community, our personal village, becomes sparse. The joy goes out of life. Our overall satisfaction with life is lower, and we do not live as long.

Today we stand at a place in history where we enjoy the benefits of our forefathers' efforts and knowledge. We have the ability to multiply our food production, our muscles, our voices, and our minds. We are now ready for the next area of amplification: our emotions.

Full emotional expression is another way of saying love. Bringing full expression to our emotions, both collectively and individually, is not as easy to grasp as manipulating physical things like food or telephones or airplanes or computers. We define our humanity by our emotions: tenderness, compassion, and generosity, to name a few of the positive ones. Emotion is the foundation for our amazing creativity. It gives us the vocabulary to describe our dreams, our visions of the future, our soul and spirit, and our awe of beauty.

Our success in balancing mechanical advances with the emotional and eventually the spiritual dimensions of life will determine how, or even if, we continue as a species. The answer will lie, as it always has, in the integrity of our communal structures. It is the framework of community that will enable us to move to that next evolutionary step, the full expression of our emotional nature—love.

Community is the container or vehicle in which our human journey unfolds. Every level of interaction from the family to a global audience happens within its context.

I like to think of community as the greenhouse in which the flower of humanity can bloom. A greenhouse is a container that shelters the plants from destructive external forces and assures that they receive adequate amounts of heat, light, food, and water. Within its protective confines, all the plants can thrive. Community does the same for people.

Abraham Maslow, a great psychologist and philosopher, observed that all people require certain basic things in order to live a full life. He started a list of universal needs that are absolutely necessary for the full expression of our humanity. Community is the nurturing container for humanity, which assures that those needs are fulfilled. Since Maslow first started his list others have expanded it, so that it now contains seven items. We will go into this in detail later, but for starters here is the list.

The Basic Universal Human Needs
- *Food, shelter, and the assurance of physical safety.*
- *A loving envelope of emotional safety.*
- *A sense of belonging.*
- *Regular touch, warmth, affection, and respect.*
- *The opportunity to be competent with our native skills.*
- *Affirmation for who we are and what we do well.*
- *Involvement in a greater transcendent meaning.*

The fulfillment of our most basic needs is not a luxury if every person in the group is to thrive. A strong community maximizes the potential that each individual will have all of these seven needs satisfied.

Just as the community benefits the individual, every person's contribution is needed for a community to thrive. All successful community systems, from the smallest to the largest, contain certain ingredients which must be present if the community is to provide the opportunity for everyone's basic needs to be satisfied to some degree.

The Essential Ingredients of a Healthy Community
- *People*
- *Common ground*
- *Committed members*
- *Trust*
- *Servant leaders*
- *Territory*
- *History*
- *Symbols, myths, and legends*
- *Effective communication systems*
- *Agreed-upon rules for behavior*
- *Rituals, celebrations, and play*
- *Sense of interdependence*

Without the containment of community, the human race would never have evolved to the high state we now enjoy. We would not now be in the place where we can dance with all the ingredients listed above. Of course volumes have been written about each of these ingredients and more volumes will be written, but for now simply note that if you are to have a successful communal experience, all of these ingredients have to be operating. In this book I will show you how to apply these ingredients in a practical way that you can use to create your own personal community.

The move toward globalization has made it imperative that we address the needs of the individual in order to maintain balance in the world. As we have moved collectively toward a global community, too often individual and local interests have been swept aside to create more efficient manufacturing, military, and monetary systems. The nation and city will not thrive if the individuals of the community—the personal villages—are not strong and thriving. The larger society and the personal villages are interdependent. The personal village is where we start.

CHAPTER 1

Revitalizing Community Is Urgent Business

Our world has changed more in the last few decades than at any other time in history. A burst of technological innovations has led to great advances, benefits that have enhanced the lives of a huge part of the population. And yet this great leap forward comes at a price and creates some peril. Historically technology has brought benefits, but it has also placed the population at a dehumanizing risk. Many forces are at work today that erode both our sense of self and our sense of being part of a larger community. Unless we find a way to balance these forces, the future looks grim. The answer lies in revitalizing community life at all levels of society. You can start by creating strong personal community circles.

We live in a vastly different world from our ancestors, our grandparents, and our parents. Even the world as we knew it five years ago is gone. It seems that everything has changed. And that change has jolted every single person on this planet. Ann who lives on Prospect Avenue in Milwaukee, Hamid who lives in the Shemiran neighborhood in Tehran, and Kung on PraArthit Road in Bangkok all ask the same question: What is happening to our world, to my community, to my life?

We can all see what has happened here in Western society.
- *Privacy—out.*
- *Speed—in.*
- *Opportunity—explosive.*
- *Fragmentation—our middle name.*
- *Consumer unit—our new identity.*
- *Community life—disintegrating.*
- *Intimacy—our longing.*
- *"Hurry—more—I want—Gimme," —our motto.*
- *Excitement, hope, frustration, and apprehension— our inner state.*
- *Information and technology—our intoxication.*

Ah, technology. What a sweet intoxicant it is for all of us. Artists use it to push the creative expression of cinema, art, music, and dance to levels that bedazzle us. Social commentators employ it to bring everyone into a worldwide conversation about human rights, public health, poverty, and social inequality. The press uses it to expose the underhanded activities of self-serving or tyrant leaders. People in underdeveloped countries long for its benefits.

Our world has changed more in the last few decades than at any time in human history.

Scientists and engineers have placed in our hands amazing new tools, which change how we cook, work, and travel. The resulting expansion has created a mini *big bang* for each of us. The discoveries and wisdom of all of human history are now available to almost every single person. Our lives are blessed. Our future has never been brighter.

Today we stand upon the foundation our ancestors built, as we multiply their discoveries many-fold. Civilized life began around

15,000 years ago when hunter-gatherer bands first settled in small settlements. Some of these grew into cities and finally, in the last 6000 years, into actual civilizations. In China, India, Persia, and all around the Mediterranean basin, great advances in technology, philosophy, religion, business, commerce, architecture, and governmental systems emerged. These advances have now spread across history and the whole planet. Collectively, our species has created a legacy of creativity that has moved us forward into a new and wonderful world.

For the first time in human history, we may actually eliminate disease, war, and poverty. The advocates of our modern condition tell us that the current information, electronic, and global age will lift us to highs that humanity has never known. There is now the potential for everyone on the planet to embrace all of humankind's entire store of information and wisdom. This world holds the promise that all of us can rise to our full potential both as individuals and as a global culture.

And yet humanity is standing at a crossroads. One fork could take us forward into prosperity, love, and greatness unimagined. The other fork could take us over a precipice.

Yes, there is a dark side to our explosive leap into the future. In our dash to embrace technology, we have brought about some unexpected side effects, which may turn out to be quite disagreeable in the long run.

> *The burst of technology has led to great advances in creativity and economic benefit for a huge number of people.*

Modern transportation has put us at risk from epidemics carried around the world in days. An avalanche of evidence points to global warming that will flood our coastlines, force massive population migrations, inundate cities, perhaps trigger another ice age, and totally disrupt the cultural and economic reality of the world as we know it. The merchandising industry, in its efforts to transform us into consuming units for the great market place, too often degrades our humanity.

Psychologists warn that the epidemic of violence in American culture is the result of flooding our youth with images of violence and disrespect for human life. Evidence is growing that exposing children to television and computers before age seven can retard, even damage, their young developing brains. Terrorists now use technology against us. The shadow of ecological destruction hovers over us like an omen of doom. Serious thinkers contend that our current prosperity is like a pyramid scheme, transferring wealth to those at the top with tremendous cost to the human soul, the disenfranchised, and future generations.

Yes, we are all excited and nervous at the same time. All of us know from history that every time technology has jerked us forward, what followed was a combination of great opportunity and disasters and, eventually, enormous benefit. Gunpowder was first seen as a great advance in warfare, then apprehended with horror when we saw what modern warfare did to real people.

The invention of global navigation brought a horde from Europe into the New World, where opportunities were boundless. But that great opportunity for the Europeans came at a terrible price. It is estimated that 50 million people lived a very civilized life in North America before that migration. Two hundred years after the Europeans arrived with their gunpowder and diseases, only one million of the First Nation people remained.

A classic, unforeseen result of technology occurred in ancient Greece. About 490 BC, Athens was becoming a thriving city. To the east, 150 miles across the Aegean Sea, lay the great Persian Empire. Xerxes, the king of Persia, decided to defeat the Athenians and add the Greek peninsula to his kingdom. When he invaded, he was met by a ragtag army of Greeks who, by pure luck, beat him back. A Greek by the name of Pericles came to power in Athens about that time. He realized that the Persians would return for a second try. Pericles had a plan. His marine engineers had designed a giant rowboat with a battering ram on the front. With 300 men rowing on a direct collision course, any boat they hit was soon fish food. They called them triremes. Triremes were the guided missile of the time.

So Pericles ordered a fleet of triremes built. When the Persians returned in their boats, these marvels of technology swarmed out and sank the entire Persian fleet.

Heady with victory and technological superiority, Pericles decided to tease the Spartans into a battle so he could take control of all of southern Greece. His plan was to attack the Spartans, then retreat behind a massive wall and carry out the war while the city was provisioned by triremes. He had the wall built so that it enclosed Athens and protected the harbor. It seemed like a secure plan, and all of Athens joined in enthusiastically. A safe sanctuary guaranteed by a steady supply of provisions from their ships seemed to assure success. Or so they believed.

At first the war went according to plan. But they did not anticipate that these very modern ships which provided supplies also would bring plague-carrying rats. A great epidemic spread through the city, from which even their high-tech triremes could not rescue them. The population was decimated. Even Pericles, the great leader and visionary, succumbed to the epidemic. The sickened city was overrun by the Spartans, who burned and pillaged it and then left for home with a stern admonition to the Athenians never to do that again.

The story of Athens has been repeated over and over throughout history. Today's technological advances have created problems never before seen on such a grand scale. Overpopulation of our planet has scientists warning that the demands of caring for all of us are resulting in soil depletion, water shortages, forest destruction, species extinction, and toxic sterilization of many important large bodies of water. Some of these same scientists project that the current trend will soon—by 2030—permanently damage the planet, damage that could degrade the quality of life for our children and take millions of years to repair. The past lessons of careless use of technology may very soon be impressed upon us again.

Already we see an epidemic of violence, fear, depression, and self-serving foolishness among the general population. Consumers who eagerly pay top dollars for new cars and fancy gadgets routinely vote down school levies; they demand lower taxes and then complain about a lack of government services. Research shows that people are spending less time with their friends. In America, civic involvement is at an all-time low. Many see the Americanization of the world as a cultural disaster. Benjamin Barber, one of the watchdogs of our society, baldly states in his book *Jihad vs. McWorld* that we are becoming "McWorld, whose noisy soul is television and MTV." A growing number of concerned people around the world are taking to the streets in alarm about the impacts of globalizing technology and short-sighted economic systems.

Some child development experts claim the entertainment and electronic game industries are training our children to show disrespect for human life and to view violence as a sport. A growing number of experts believe that the epidemic of violence has its roots in a profound miscarriage of the mother-infant bond, brought about by our collective failure to support motherhood.

> *Unless we find a way to counterbalance the negative tides of technology, the future looks grim.*

Whatever the cause, it is clear that our modern world has unleashed forces which, in spite of great benefits, act to degrade the quality of life in our communities, alienate us from our close intimates, and, indeed, corrode the inner recesses of our private lives. Let me suggest a few more.

Too many options: An overabundance of choices can create a level of activity that crowds out leisure time and overwhelms us.

Information overload: The information we have is a good thing, but too much information can crowd out space inside of us for our friends, our family, and ourselves.

Hurry-hurry: Our habit of hurrying often leads to impatience with the simple process of spending time with our intimates or in nature.

Aggressive advertising: Advertising fuels an illusion that life is about instant gratification and intensity. It does not lead us toward the deep connection with our fellows for which we all long.

Mobility: With increased mobility we have simply picked up and moved away from each other. We have become scattered. One of the essential ingredients for a satisfying community is stability of place.

Centralized manufacture and distribution of goods: We have more products than we ever imagined possible and at unbelievable prices. But gone are Mom and Pop at the corner grocery store who knew us personally.

Many other things act to interrupt our personal and communal lives, but we hear about them every day in the news so I won't go on. The question stands: What is to be done to balance the forces at work in our world, to assure that this epoch in human history is a step forward?

THERE IS AN ANSWER

The answer lies in our evolutionary history. All through our evolution we have lived, loved, and died within the sheltering embrace of community. In community we created villages and cities and civilizations and technology and medicine and philosophy and religion. In community we held a respect for Mother Earth. In community we collectively honored that greater thing variously called God, Allah, Shiva, or Great Spirit. In community we learned how to be respectful to each other. In community we sheltered our babies and cared for the infirm. In community we cultivated ideas that today have bloomed into the fertile garden in which we now live. And it will be in community that we will create a solution to the problems of our new world.

The clarion call to revitalize community is being heard from every corner of the land. Community has many expressions. You will find it in church, on the streets, at work, in special interest groups, in cities, in nations, and even in the global family. But for the average person, community really happens up close with the people most often encountered: our personal village. We all need to create, revitalize, and maintain the circles of people around us, as we dance together collectively in a wonderful world sometimes gone crazy.

This is urgent business. The task of rebuilding community falls to every single individual, as well as to our civic leaders and the captains of industry. Our survival as a race depends upon revitalizing our personal communities, our personal villages. Ultimately, it is up to each of us to have a strong core community. So far, I have been talking about our culture in general. It is now time to turn our attention to the personal village as a universal institution passed down through history, and to explore why it is so important to each one of us.

> *The answer lies in revitalizing community life at all levels of society.*

In Summary

- Civilization has changed more in the last few decades than at any time in human history.

- A burst of technological innovations has led to great advances, benefits which have enhanced the lives of a huge part of the population.

- Historically, technology has brought both benefits and great tragedies, placing us at risk of degrading our humanity.

- Many forces are at work that erode our sense of self and community.

- Too many options create confusion.

- Information overload floods our brains.

- Inhumane speed causes physical and psychological stress.

- Aggressive advertising distorts reality.

- Mobility shatters our stable community sense.

- Centralized manufacturing and distribution of goods degrades small community-based businesses.

- If we find a way to balance the forces that impact the health of our individual personal villages, we increase the likelihood that we will achieve the promise of our potential and not the decline of our worst fears.

- The answer lies in revitalizing community life at all levels of society.

- The place to start is by creating strong, personal community circles.

RESOURCES YOU CAN USE

Future Shock by Alvin Toffler, 1970

> This classic has been read and re-read by leaders all over the world in an attempt to get a glimpse into what the future holds. It is eerie how the predictions that Toffler made in 1970 have all come true. This book and the subsequent books he wrote are well worth digesting.

High Tech • High Touch by John Nasbitt, 1999

> Nasbitt lays out in everyday language the challenges facing all of us in modern life, and calls for a restoration of "high touch" to bring us back into balance. By *high touch* he means a high level of authentic human contact.

Jihad vs. McWorld: How Globalism and Tribalism Are Reshaping the World by Benjamin Barber, 1996

> Read this book if you want to know why people in the United States are uneasy, and why the rest of the world is in an uproar about the spread of capitalism and so-called American values. Written in an easy-to-read style, this book explores the collision between human nature, technology, and economic change, as globalism becomes a fact of life. If you read only one book on this list, make it this one.

Bowling Alone by Robert Putnam, 2000

> Putnam is a social scientist who pulled all the research together to describe the collapse of civil society in America. He makes some suggestions about how to correct the problem at a larger social level.

Guns, Germs, and Steel: The Fates of Human Society by Jared Diamond, 1998

> The winner of a Pulitzer Prize, this magnificent book is due to become a classic. Diamond describes the rise of human society from hunter-gatherer to the civilizations we enjoy today. He outlines very clearly how and why we became what we are today.

Avalon, a film featuring Armin Mueller-Stahl, Elizabeth Perkins, and Aidan Quinn, 1990

> A delightful tale about a Jewish immigrant from the old country who finds community and prosperity in his new home, America. From that happy beginning we watch the gradual decay of community, a decay that comes from the collision between old, established community structures which no longer work, urban sprawl, and the dissipation of his family and close loved ones into the landscape of American opportunity. It's happy, funny, and poignant.

Koyaanisqatsi, a film conceived, produced, and directed by Godfrey Reggio, 1983

> Koyaanisqatsi (ko yaa nis qatsi) is from the Hopi language. It means 1) a crazy life; 2) life in turmoil; 3) life out of balance; 4) life disintegrating; or 5) a state of life that calls for another way of living. This beautiful visual essay with a magnificent sound track brings into clear perspective the importance of staying in harmony with ourselves and Mother Earth if we are to retain our humanity. It is a powerful classic.

CHAPTER 2

Personal Village
The Most Valuable Asset In Your Life

Your personal village includes every single person you know. It is continually changing and growing. If you approach it with a plan, it will become the most valuable asset in your life. The human story is one of people bonding together to give each other help. With the increasing clamor of the modern world, it becomes important that each of us nurture a personal village: a place where we can rest our hearts in the embrace of the community of people who populate our immediate lives.

No matter where you are, you live in a village—a village that contains the entire host of people who make up the fabric of your life. It is not a village in the classic sense of thatched roofs, cows, and dusty roads, but rather a human village that contains all of the people who, just as in the ideal villages of old, shelter you with warmth, caring, security, and a sense of belonging and purpose.

This specific constellation of people which is the very root of your life is unique to you, and to no one else. This collection of people is your personal village.

Your personal village is one of the most important assets you will ever have in your life. Why is it so important? The answer is simple. Every single thing you will need to live your life to its fullest potential involves people: elders to raise you, educational and career opportunities, the richness of your own adult family, spiritual evolution, health care, financial resources, chances to reach your highest potential, and support as you age and become infirm. These people populate your personal village. If your village is sparse, your life will probably be empty and lacking. If, on the other hand, you succeed in filling your village with a host of supportive people, your life will be full and rich. There is a one-to-one correlation between the strength of your personal village and the success of your life.

No matter where you are, you live in a village that contains the entire host of people who make up the fabric of your life.

Every person you know is a member of your personal village, and each of them has his or her own personal village. You are connected to each person you know. Some of these connections are single-stranded: the person is linked to you but to no one else in your personal village. However, most of the people in your life are linked not only to you but to others that you both know. These multiple connections bring many of the people in your personal village together, and then link them to even more people. The resulting network is like a gigantic intertwining of spider webs. At the middle of each web is a personal village, centered on one individual. These tiny centers of humanity are the base unit of society.

Each personal village is unique, and it does not happen by chance. For a long time I lived in my personal village by default. I let people come and go without any awareness that I could have something to do about their being there. People came and went. I liked many of them and thrived on the wisdom and resources they had to offer. But I had not learned the lessons of purposefulness or the virtues of gratefulness, reciprocity, and kindness. So these people drifted away and I was lonely. Then new ones came along and I was happy. Then they drifted away because I did not tend to the relationships and I was lonely again. So it went.

During this period of cycling between loneliness and happiness, I met someone who would show me the value of deliberately creating community. Al was my engineering supervisor at a large industrial corporation. He adopted me and once again I was happy. People from every level of the corporation seemed to know Al. There was always someone dropping by his desk to visit. I noticed that not only would he always introduce me to these people but also that he always ended the conversation with the comment, "Be sure to take care of your friends."

One day Al invited me to his birthday party. To my surprise, in attendance were all the people whom I had watched troop past his desk over the last two years. At the final toast, Al again reminded us to take care of each other.

After that party, I asked him what he meant by "Remember your friends." In answer to my question, he told me an interesting story about Robert McNamara, a very successful man, Harvard graduate, Lieutenant Colonel in the US Air Force, and eventually head of the Ford Motor Company. Al maintained that when McNamara went to work for Ford, he made a pact with several of his colleagues to help each other succeed in their work. At the time Al told me this story, McNamara had moved on and was serving as head of the World Bank. Later he served as secretary of defense during the Vietnam War era. Some question the policies and decisions that he made in his career, but no one can deny that McNamara was very effective at how he went about his work.

Al maintained that it was McNamara's strategic approach with the people around him that had contributed to his ability to be professionally and politically successful. He also pointed out that without the support of your friends in a large company, you would never go anywhere. It is the mutual agreement between a small group of people that opens doors and leads to opportunities. Al had taught me the basics of how to create and work a network.

Later, I left the engineering profession and went back to graduate school to study social work. Several years had passed when I received a call from Al. His daughter had been killed and he was now housebound with emphysema. Would I please come to see him? In his hour of need, Al was calling in some of his social capital. I had no choice; every cell in my body pulled me to his side. When his wife let me into the house, I found Al hunched over in a chair, gray with illness, an oxygen tube in his nose, and very depressed.

> *You can either drift along by default or be purposeful and build a community that will work for you.*

We talked and cried, and he told me that all his friends from the company had come to see him. He felt their support was the only thing that was carrying him through this difficult time. I never saw him again, as he died soon after our time together.

That final meeting with Al left a deep impression burned into my heart. At first I had been put off by the idea of a purposeful agreement to band together, because it implied shutting some people out. Then I realized that this is what we do naturally, all the time. We trust the people we know, we turn to them for resources, help, advice, and opportunities, and we offer them the same. The social psychologists call the result *social capital*. Everyone agrees to put energy into the relationship and the social capital grows. Then when we are in need we draw some out. We do this in all of our relationships: in families, fellowships, support groups, friendships, and business. That is how the world works. That is how the world has always worked. And that is how the world will always work.

When I applied the lesson of deliberately creating community to my personal life, it worked. Before long, I was connected to my neighbors, I had a close circle of trusted friends, I had a weekly support group where I could really be myself, and I had an expanding circle of colleagues to support my career. Gone was the hit-and-miss approach to relationships. I was learning how to live my social life purposefully and with a plan. Over the past forty years, I have multiplied the original lesson Al taught me many times over. The first principle I learned about developing my personal community was to be purposeful. It is important to be proactive and to make your people circles happen, rather than wait for chance to bring people into your life.

The second principle I learned was to have a plan.

HANG OUT WHERE PEOPLE DO THINGS THAT INTEREST YOU

Marie grew up with parents who understood the art of creating a strong personal village.

She had learned her lessons well and was practiced at surrounding herself with warm and caring people. When she moved away from home to attend college in a distant city, she was all alone. Since she did not live on campus, the ready-made community of a dormitory or sorority was not available. So she began to hang out at a nearby coffee shop-bakery.

Every day Marie was there, studying and talking with people. She treated it like her second home. In time she began to meet the other regulars, and soon she had a large net of casual acquaintances. She could go there almost any time and see someone she knew. She could always find someone who was interested in talking or going to a movie or taking a walk.

Later she took a part-time job as a receptionist at a health club. That put Marie in a position to meet lots of the same people every week. At first these people were strangers to her but soon they became familiar strangers and later casual acquaintances. Two even became friends. The job put her with people who shared her interest in physical fitness and, since she was allowed to work out after hours with the rest of the staff, she had a natural way to interact with them. She was purposeful in creating opportunities for contact with others. Those interactions developed a sense of belonging within a circle of people with a shared common interest. Marie followed the strategy of hanging out in the territory where people were doing the things that were of interest to her.

The idea of being purposeful in creating immediate community support is not new. Most students of community dynamics point to the work of a remarkable naturalist and Russian prince, Peter Kropotkin. In the late 1800s he described the universal human process of banding together to create community. His classic book *Mutual Aid* described how most species, and humans in particular, have a very rich pattern of cooperation. Kropotkin pointed out that within the boundaries of their immediate group, people have always engaged in various forms of sharing, mutual aid, and celebration of life. Of course, there has always been self-centeredness, competition, senseless violence, greed, and, at the boundary of the group, war. And yet at the same time, the value we have placed on community and cooperation has always been strong.

In preindustrial European cultures, the guild tradition even spelled out this cooperation as a condition of belonging. Kropotkin described the code of a Danish Guild in 1785.

> The social duties of the brethren were enumerated: If a brother's house was burned, or he lost his ship, or suffered on a pilgrim's voyage, all the brethren must come to his aid. If a brother fell dangerously ill, two brethren must keep watch by his bed until he was out of danger. If he died, the brethren must prepare his body, then follow him to the church and the grave. After his death they must assure that his children were provided for. Very often the widow became a sister to the guild.

Kropotkin also described how in pre-Revolutionary Russia, gathering together in mutual-aid clusters was an ingrained part of the culture. These clusters, or *artels* as they were called, formed around any shared activity.

When ten or twenty peasants traveled away from their village to work as weavers, carpenters, or boat-builders, they would always form an artel. They secured rooms, hired a cook, elected an elder, and took their meals in common, each paying the artel his share for food and lodging. The concept of forming a cooperative group was a natural part of their lives, so much so that when a party of convicts was sent to Siberia, they formed an artel, with an elected elder serving as the officially recognized intermediary between the convicts and their jailer. These same clusters were formed to provide a community structure for the prisoners when they reached the hard labor camps. The idea of artel was deeply embedded in the psyche of most Russians during that period. It was a concept that helped bind them together as a people.

This same concept developed in the village culture of Eastern European Jews. Their rich collective life evolved over several hundred years into a village form, where everyone had a place and everyone supported everyone else. These communities were called *shtetls*. A romanticized version of a shtetl village was the inspiration for the musical *Fiddler on the Roof*. Though tragically the shtetl disappeared during World War II, most of us in Western civilization are still influenced by the idealized village concept that culture came to represent. The memory of a people-centered shtetl is still used as a blueprint for what is possible in community.

Banding together is an ancient human practice.

Artels and shtetls are only two of the many kinds of successful community forms. Unfortunately, the demise of these two preindustrial institutions marked the end of an era. That era was a time when agreements for providing support, evolved over thousands of years, were well established and deeply ingrained in everyone. With the two world wars and the advent of technology all of this has changed, and a serious loss of human contact has resulted. The community forms by which people once found nurturing human contact in their daily lives do not work very well in modern society. But if we work together collectively, we can find a way to make the timeless forms of mutual aid and community function in a world racing toward globalization.

Many successful community systems have sprung up. You find them as neighborhood coalitions, church congregations, business associations, city governments, and even as organizations that operate at the international level. But these communities offer only a partial antidote to the loneliness, alienation, and soul-stripping consumerism that our frantic world force-feeds us. To cope with this bombardment effectively, we must look to our personal villages for the answers. We must initiate, cultivate, and participate in the process of revitalizing the natural forms of face-to-face contact found within our most immediate circles.

To experience nourishing forms of contact can be as simple as saying hello to your neighbor or greeting the grocery cashier. In your personal village you can have true intimacy and belonging. The computer banks may have all your private information, but in your intimate circles you will always have privacy and an escape from the noise and the hurry (especially if you also turn off your phone, your television, and your computer). As you strengthen your personal village, you will find it easier to balance your life as we all race headlong into the future. Consider it your private garden where you can go to rest your heart and replenish your soul.

> *Your personal village is one of the few places to find privacy and to escape from the mind-numbing stimulation of modern life.*

A well-tended garden nurtures and refreshes everyone who walks its paths. The same is true for a person with a healthy personal village. A garden changes constantly with the seasons, and so does a village. The gardener has to work hard planning and planting, digging and weeding, watering and fertilizing. Then the garden produces blooms, fruit, shade, and solace for both the gardener and its visitors. The personal village requires the same amount of work and provides a similar degree of comfort, solace, and stimulation. There is a certain energy that springs from true contact with other people. Our personal villages can be rich centers, pulsating with energy. Just like in a garden, some of that life force is tangible to the hand, eye, and nose. But there is also a part that we can only sense, an invisible pulsation of life that emanates from our gardens and villages, a life force that nourishes, calms, and restores us. The multiple circles of people who populate our personal villages fill our psychic gardens with energy and provide reserves we can draw from to live full and happy lives.

Just as each garden is different, so is every individual's personal village. Your personal village includes everyone you know. It includes your family, your friends, your associates, and all of the separate and diverse people who support your life: the banker, the doctor, the grocery store clerk, and the familiar strangers you recognize but don't know. And at the very center of every personal village is the single most important person of all—you.

Interaction with people at every level of your personal village is nourishing both to you and to everyone you encounter. The grocery store clerk is only a familiar stranger, but seeing her briefly every week sparks a feeling of comfort and belonging in that place for both of you. The neighbors may be strangers, but greeting them occasionally gives a subtle sense of depth to your walk-around community. The privacy of a therapy or support group offers a totally different level of trust and intimacy, which increases your creativity, improves your health, and helps you live longer. The casual interaction of the people at work, although few of them are close friends, provides a sense of place and support for your productivity that is more valuable than gold. Sharing with a close confidant or immediate family member is food for the souls of both of you.

Of course this may sound idealistic. Perhaps you do not experience this at all. But it is possible, and for many people it is the reality of their lives. It can be your reality too if you put energy into making it happen. Failure to be purposeful and proactive in nourishing your personal village is what I mean by living your life by default.

We all know people who live their lives by default. They never balance their checkbooks or develop a plan for their money or career or health. Sometimes they stumble into success, but more often than not these defaulters end up in a pickle. You may end up alone if you choreograph your relationships by default. If you do not return phone calls or reach out to people or actively work to nourish your relationships, you need this book.

There is a one-to-one correlation between the strength of your personal village and the success of your life.

Your personal village is where you will find intimacy. Intimacy—such an illusive concept. Most people want it but do not have a clear idea of what it is or how it works. Before I take you into the details of how to make your village work, I want to orient you to the way I think about intimacy. This next chapter on intimacy lays a foundation for the rest of the book. Every relationship you have will fall somewhere on the intimacy continuum.

IN SUMMARY

- Your personal village includes everyone you know. It is continually changing.

- Your personal village is one of the most important assets you will have in your life.

- The first two principles you will need to apply in order to assure a strong personal village for yourself are a) to be purposeful in your relationships and b) to think strategically.

- The first strategy in creating community is to hang out with people who are doing things that interest you.

- Bonding together in purposeful communities is as old as humanity.

- Your personal village is the only place to get real comfort and to escape the mind-numbing stimulation of modern life.

- A strong personal village will require continual attention and renewal.

RESOURCES YOU CAN USE

Life is With People: The Culture of the Shtetl by Mark Zborowski and Elizabeth Herzog, 1952

> At the end of World War II, a group of American anthropologists realized that the stable village culture of the Eastern European Jews had ended. They launched a research project to interview the survivors of that way of life before they died off and it was forgotten. This classic about a vanished culture is the synthesis of their research. It is a jewel of a book describing humanity and a highly evolved, rich community life.

Mutual Aid by Peter Kropotkin. First published in 1902 and still available

> Every study of small groups and mutual support refers to this classic. Kropotkin was a brilliant Russian prince who recognized the organic need for people in community to make a conscious effort to help each other. His description of a society in another time and place teaches us that mutual assistance is universal in the human story.

The Shelter of Each Other: Rebuilding Our Families by Mary Pipher, Ph.D., 1996

> Full of heart, tenderness, and warmth, this book is a passionate call to restore community within the family. It is all about personal villages in the context of family. I strongly recommend you imbibe the wisdom Pipher offers in her book.

The Healing Web: Social Networks and Human Survival
by Marc Pilisuk and Susan Hillier Parks, 1986

> The most definitive book about communities that I have
> ever read. Comprehensive and filled with references, it
> is the academic equivalent of the book you hold in your
> hands.

Fiddler on the Roof, a musical filmed in 1971 starring Tutte
Lemkow

> This classic film depicting a romanticized version of shtetl
> life brought tears to the eyes of the people who had once
> lived in those villages because, as they said, "That's just
> how life was." It shows the delights and struggles of Tevye,
> a poor milkman who lives surrounded by his personal vil-
> lage in the shtetl. It is a magnificent work showing life in
> all its dimensions, from simple to complex, ever changing,
> ever rich, fully human.

CHAPTER 3

Where Is The Intimacy?

We need to be in harmony with each other to regulate our internal body rhythms, and that is why we are communal creatures. Intimacy is that soul-nourishing interaction with others which we find in just a few places. Intimacy takes time and effort to develop, and it happens only when people let down their guard and allow others to know who they truly are. We do not have time in our lives for very many of these relationships, so we need to be selective. Most relationships are low on intimacy and high on affiliation, meaning we share something in common but not the depth of knowing the very heart of each other. If you think of intimacy as a measurable experience and place it on a continuum within your personal village, you will discover that you can adjust the level of intimacy you experience with others, varying it from anonymity to affiliation to true, heart-warming interweaving with another.

Have you ever wondered why humans need community so much? Many scientists have puzzled over this. Social scientists have known for decades that when people are embedded in a strong community system, everything goes better for everyone. People live longer. They are healthier, and when they get sick, they get well faster. When community is strong, people seem to thrive and are more creative and inventive.

Certainly the ancient Greeks realized the value of community, if the words of Plato are any indication. His classic *The Republic* is a long discussion on the value of community and how it should work. But the early Greeks merely recognized its importance, they did not understand why it is so necessary. Generally we just take community for granted as if it were a given; few of us even think about it.

However, scientists are only the latest to take up the ancient questions about the nature of love and human contact and why it is so important. Why are teenagers so eager to be together? Why are men and women driven to team up briefly or for life? Why do people gather into families and towns and cities and nations, interwoven with a complex net of interactions? Why do friendships thrive? Why do babies need their mothers so intensely? Why do the elderly thrive when they are with others?

For a long time it was thought that the major reason we evolved into communal creatures was the need to band together for mutual protection against predators and external dangers. If we did not take care of our babies and children, there would be no one around to carry the gene pool forward. So scientists concluded that we are genetically driven to be communal in order to make sure the next generation survives long enough to make more copies of themselves. The need to band together for mutual protection and the need to care for our young cooperatively seemed to explain why we are communal creatures. This explanation held until scientists developed instruments that could record what happens inside the body and the brain. Then some very interesting things emerged. There was more to it than was first believed.

In one study, scientists wired up mothers and their infants who were in close physical contact, and they watched what was happening to the heart rate, breathing rate, brain waves, and body chemistry. To their surprise, they discovered that these two people seemed to be almost perfectly entrained to each other. When the mother's heart rate increased, so did the baby's. When mother got sleepy, so did baby. When mother was calm, baby's body chemistry registered calmness. When mother was upset, baby's body chemistry and brain waves indicated it was upset also.

It appeared that these mother-infant pairs were totally in tune with each other, as if they were one person. Gradually these scientists began to recognize that the mother's presence, her smell, the sound of her voice, and the quality of her touch were teaching her baby's inner regulatory mechanisms how to work. A baby entrained on its mother's state; this entrainment enabled the baby's brain to grow in positive ways and helped to regulate all the health producing mechanisms in the developing child. At the same time, the mother showed evidence that she too was benefiting from being in close contact with her baby. The entrainment worked to smooth out her inner state, and that allowed her to be more attentive to her baby.

Scientists call this state *limbic resonance*, meaning that the emotional brains of these two people are in harmony. Once the infant learns how to become self-regulating—by patterning its inner processes on its mother, and later on its father, and eventually on the whole host of people who care for it—the baby develops the ability to keeps its brain waves, body rhythms, and body chemistry in a smooth state all by itself. At least for a while; the baby needs to come back to its mother from time to time for a harmonizing fix, to keep its inner state stable.

> *The company of others allows us to stay in balance within ourselves. That is why we need community.*

It is now well known that an infant needs the close contact of its mother and of others for its neurological architecture to develop in a positive way.

The need for limbic resonance applies not only to babies and mothers, but to all of us. We need some contact with others to keep our hormones in a positive range, to keep our hearts beating smoothly, to maintain a strong immune system, and to have a sense of well-being.

You can call it getting your people fix or limbic resonance or hanging out together, but the end result is the same. We need each other to maintain our inner harmony. That is why we need community. It is built into our brains to thrive when we are in close interaction with people. When we do not have enough significant interaction with others, every system in our bodies and also our emotional well-being falters. Community is at the core of what it is to be human. Community is the key to surviving and thriving as alive, creative human beings.

When we are known by another we are comforted, and we drop into harmony with those who know us and with those whom we know. Being in harmony with another is intimacy.

Intimacy, that elusive something—much talked about, much sought after, and the source of so much heartache—just what is it and where is it to be found?

Valentine Michael Smith was the master of intimacy. He had an uncanny way of dropping into total harmony with others. Every man or woman who met him became totally enamored with his ability to totally know and connect with their innermost center. Valentine was raised as a Martian.

The lesson he brought from Mars was the art of *grokking*. We meet Valentine in Robert Heinlein's classic science fiction book *Stranger in a Strange Land*. In that book we meet the idea that the ability to grok is at the very heart of intimacy. Grok is a strange word to our ears. It sounds like something you would drink on a cold night, but in reality it is a word Heinlein created to capture the experience of knowing anything, including another person, so deeply that it is as if the inner experience of another individual is your own. Heinlein intended the word to sound alien because, after all, he was writing a science fiction story. And indeed it does sound alien. But alien or not, it is the only word that has appeared in the English language, or in most other languages for that matter, which captures knowing another totally, as if you were that person.

When a concept is not well understood in a culture, the language will reflect this lack by not developing words for the idea. It is as if the idea of knowing another completely is not fully developed in our culture, and thus no adequate words have evolved in the Western world, from ancient Greece up to current times, to capture the idea—until Heinlein came along. We have words like empathy and rapport and compassion, but these only partly describe what is going on between two people. When scientists saw complete harmony between the vital signs of two people, they were measuring grokking.

We have to go to the ancient Sanskrit language to find equivalent words. One such word is *aparokshajana,* which means a direct understanding of a situation, person, or thing without using any of the five senses. And several hundred years ago a yogic mystic, Patanjali, talked about the notion of *prajna,* which is a kind of direct knowledge attained through the deepest state of meditation.

In Chinese we find a word that comes close to grok. Difficult for our Western tongues to pronounce, it sounds approximately like *zi ying,* which, roughly translated, is to know the song that sings in the heart of another as if it were our own song. The Japanese language contains almost the same word, meaning to know the heart of another without using words. Though many people are put off by the harsh sound of grok, it has found its way into the English language. The idea of totally knowing another is apparently still quite new in our self-oriented culture,

> *To grok someone is to embrace the experience of knowing them so deeply that it is as if their inner experience is your own.*

given that even the dictionary definitions are quite feeble compared to the depth of meaning that Heinlein intended. Yet the concept of totally knowing another person, situation, or idea in the very deepest way is so central to good human relationships that, lacking another word in the contemporary Western languages, we will follow Heinlein's lead and use grok throughout this book.

Of course almost no one, save a very highly evolved spiritual being or a Martian, can grok totally. But we can grok in part, about some things, with a few people. A baby does a pretty good job of grokking its mother, and lovers are able to do it for a short time. It is as if there were a spectrum. The higher we move along the spectrum of grokking, the more intimacy we will have with others. Most of us can only hold up the ideal of grokking as a goal, which we are well advised to move toward in our relationships.

Ceci Miller, a fellow writer and close friend, once wrote:
*As a teenager I had the goal of becoming a good listener.
I considered it one of life's greatest skills and knew that it
required practice to develop. I noticed, when listening to
others, that I usually got involved in some intriguing line
of thought, at which point I could no longer hear what was
said. Worse, sometimes I interrupted the other person to
announce what great thoughts I was having! This pretend-
listening, as I waited to voice my ideas, went on for years.*

Ceci recognized as a young woman that she had not yet learned how to listen totally, thereby precluding the possibility of grokking. To achieve intimacy with another, we have to begin by listening. This means we have to set aside our own inner voice long enough to hear the other person totally—their words, their feelings, their hopes, their dreams and disappointments, their pain and their joy. By listening we come to know another, and intimacy grows from the ground of this knowledge.

The deepest level of intimacy occurs between two people who are able to grok (know) each other. But realize that very few of our relationships will be this intimate. Most of the people we interact with fall somewhere in the middle, between the complete anonymity of a stranger and the total intimacy of our most cherished others. For the most part, the people of our personal villages are those we affiliate with in some way but don't know well enough to grok to any degree. The majority of our various affiliations are based on the sharing of common elements. We can have common ground without knowing much about the inner experience of others. The language of intimacy shows that there is a continuum of intimacy. We all move back and forth upon that continuum.

THE INTIMACY CONTINUUM

The word *intimacy* has its roots in the Latin word *intimus*, meaning *most within*. Intimacy refers to being deeply within the psychic space of another. The more we drink in the inner experience of the other, the more intimate we become with them.

Inner assumes that there is an *outer*, and Latin has a word for that too. It is *extrus*, which means *outside* or *external*. And between these two is *intus*, the Latin for *within*. When we put these Latin words together we get a continuum of intimacy: from external to most within.

 **Extus** *(external)* *(a stranger)*  **Intus** *(within)* *(a known person, an affiliate)*  **Intimus** *(most within)* *(an intimate)*

Perhaps you have already noticed that intimacy happens along a continuum. You will always find yourself someplace along this continuum, depending upon your company. Most of your relationships will be on the low end of intimacy, and a select few will be at the most intimate or inner part of your personal experience. Most of your connections with the people in your personal village will lie someplace in between. You will move back and forth along this continuum as you interact with a wide variety of people. Below is what the continuum looks like for the average personal village.

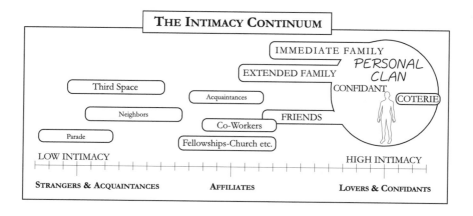

REAL INTIMACY GROWS OUT OF RELATIONSHIP

Where does intimacy start? As we have seen, it starts in the entrained relationship between a mother and an infant where, in effect, the two of them are so connected they are essentially one. Gradually the child begins to move toward more and more independence, as a sense of self grows inside. But that growing sense of self is always in relation to everyone around the child. For the first ten or fifteen years of life, we tend to define ourselves by other people: first our parents, then our teachers and media stars. In our teens we turn to our peers to find values, ways of being, and appropriate behaviors. We learn how to be by identifying with these influential people. Eventually, if we have good teachers, we grow to have a sense of our own ideas, worth, and direction. This progression takes us through a long evolution from dependence to self-dependence, and it all happens in the context of interacting with others.

You know the journey well. We are delighted and sometimes frustrated with the two-year-old who says "No-no-no" to everything. By the time that two-year-old is 13, he or she is saying, "Get out of my life, and drop me off at the mall on the way. And be sure to pick me up in time for dinner." The journey toward self-dependence has its moments.

As we grow, most of us arrive at a true sense of who we are. We become truly self-dependent. At the self-dependent stage of our development, we know ourselves, and our values gradually begin to reside inside us, but in reality this sense of self had its origin in the reflections of those who taught us how to be who we are.

Our evolution is helped by the love of the important people in our lives, spiritual practice, and a few good role models who teach us how to know ourselves as we identify with their wisdom and experience. As we grow into self-validating individuals, we have a foundation upon which to stand. Only then can we truly reach out to others and know them fully. After we have evolved a deep sense of ourselves as strong and resourceful people, we are ready to enter fully into truly interdependent and intimate relationships.

If we fail to traverse this evolutionary journey, at least to some extent, intimacy can remain an experience of over-dependence on others or of defining ourselves by others. Psychologists use the word *fused* to describe this state of not being able to know the difference between self and other.

The great philosophers and spiritual sages of history teach that we are all connected in some profound way. Some call that connection the true meaning of divinity. When we are connected with ourselves, we are connected with everyone else at some level. When we experience that connection or harmony with others, we call it intimacy.

DIVERSIFY! DIVERSIFY! DIVERSIFY!

Diversification is a basic principle for managing every aspect of your life. Let me explain. In order to have optimum health, you need to include a wide variety of foods in your diet: grains, dairy, meat, vegetables, fruit, ice cream. A good financial planner will tell you to place your money into many different assets. Then if one goes bad, you always have the others to fall back on. People divide their assets into physical property like real estate or antiques, and into a wide variety of stocks, bonds, cash holdings, etc. The same is true for your personal village.

As you tend your personal village, make room for a few intimate relationships and gatherings, but also roam in your neighborhood and nurture a variety of relationships in the middle of the intimacy continuum. Make sure that many of the people you know and network with do not know each other. That way if trouble emerges within one of your groups or within a relationship, you will have others to turn to who have no vested interest in the troubled circle or relationship. Those non-vested people can be a great resource to you at such times.

> *Develop relationships with people who do not know each other. Then when things go wrong, you have others to seek out for support.*

A vulnerable—perhaps precarious—personal village is one where everyone knows everyone else, does the same thing, holds the same values, or lives in the same place. In Alaska there is a village of Russians who fled the oppression of their homeland to find freedom. They brought with them all of the old ways, including the view that women are subservient to men. The young girls are pressed into marriage very early, soon pregnant, and sentenced to a life of childcare and servitude to their husbands. If a woman wants to expand the dimensions of her life outside of the traditional ways, she must flee and live her life as an outcast from the village. She is either totally in or totally out. This all-or-nothing scenario seriously limits everyone's options.

In that village there is no diversity. If this happens in your personal village, the result is an environment that can be very limiting, even psychologically dangerous.

One social scientist, Mark Granovetter, made a surprising discovery while studying people going through major changes in their lives. It turns out that distant acquaintances, those who rotate in a different sphere from you, are often as much or more help than your more intimate friends and relatives. This could be true because the more distant people have access to resources that you have not yet discovered. When your life is going through a major change, such as death or divorce or job loss, include the less intimate part of your personal village as part of your support system. You'll open up new possibilities that were not previously available to you.

THE IMPORTANCE OF CONTEXT

You have probably noticed that you can have a certain degree of intimacy with a person in one setting, but someplace else or in the company of different people, it changes. The professionals explain this by saying that it all depends upon the context. To understand this, we have to go back to Latin. *Context* comes from the Latin word *contexere,* which means to weave together. We are woven together in a way that changes as we move around.

We are woven together in ways that change as we move from one setting to another.

David has been one of my confidants for several decades. Every week we meet with a group of fellow psychotherapists to discuss our cases and our lives. He and I know everything about each other, love each other dearly, and enjoy that citadel of total privacy. We laugh together, cry together, get cranky together, and stimulate each other's intellects. We grok each other. He is one of the closest men in my life.

Yet when we are out in public, we do not know how to be with the huge intimacy that exists between us. The total context for our relationship is in professional training seminars and our weekly closed-group meeting—our coterie. A coterie is a small group of people who are committed to meet regularly and give one another support. Those seminars and our coterie weave us together. They provide the context in which David and I carry out the business of our relationship.

Sometimes people attend an intense weekend workshop and share with each other at a deep, emotional level. A very rapid intimacy develops in the context of the workshop, where they swear that they will be blood brothers forever. But if they meet on the street the next Tuesday morning, they will not know what to do with each other. The total context for their relationship was the short burst of intensity at the workshop. This is what Ralph Keys, in his book *We, the Lonely People, Searching for Community* called "the handy-dispose community."

Two people sharing a harrowing week in a life-threatening situation can also feel an intense sense of intimacy that may last a lifetime. Intimacy can develop between people very quickly if an intense emotional experience anchors them together. You could say that they came to know each other during the experience. But real intimacy is an intense, devoted, committed, heart-felt connection that happens over time.

Intimacy increases in direct proportion to the amount of personal sharing between two people. Both have to share. Both have to listen.

Throughout this book, I will show you how to shape the context of your interactions along the intimacy continuum so you can guide yourself toward any desired level of intimacy, in any setting.

Building Intimacy

You have probably figured this out by now, but just to make the point clear: Intimacy will increase in direct proportion to the degree of personal sharing that occurs between people. Intimacy will increase when you spend a lot of time with someone and share a significant amount about your inner personal life. The less time you spend together and the less you share about yourself, the lower the intimacy.

If you want intimacy to grow, spend time together. Learn the other person's scent, the sound of his voice, what she likes and does not like. Learn his hopes and dreams and disappointments. Intimacy will grow as you learn to pace your level of self-disclosure to match what is appropriate to your time together and to the context of your relationship.

A mother and infant are intimate. A husband and wife can be intimate, and it is hoped that they are. Confidants are intimate. It is possible to enter very quickly into an intimate relationship, but the most satisfying intimate relationships are rare and take a long time to develop.

True Intimacy Takes Time And Effort

Truly intimate long-term relationships have been tempered in the fire of disappointment, adversity, time, and commitment. Long after the first blush has gone out of a friendship or partnership, what is left is a legacy of trust, shared events, rituals, and the sense of being at home with each other.

Phenylethylamine (PEA) is the love chemical. When a person falls in love PEA is released into the bloodstream. It is a natural amphetamine that revs up the brain and other centers in the body, and causes two people who have fallen in love to become totally obsessed with each other. They cannot think of anyone else. They know absolutely that this is the right relationship for them, and that the problems that beset most people over time will never happen to them. They are in love. After a period of time ranging from a few weeks to, at most, three years, this hormone wears off and they fall into reality. If they got married during this time, they will begin to suffer the normal disappointments, neurotic entanglements, and annoyances that are the meat and potatoes of all relationships. If they were smart enough during this love phase to begin the work of accepting each other's differences and annoying traits, then the relationship can move on. If not, they may jump bed and move onto the next PEA high, or worse, torture each other with blame, neglect, and sometimes tyranny.

We cannot have many truly intimate relationships in our personal village because they take so much time and emotional energy. If we are lucky we will have the closeness of our immediate family, a few friends, and a coterie or two—seldom more than a total of ten to fifteen people. This is the collection of people that sociologists call our *sympathy circle*. We simply do not have time in our lives for more. However there are other places to have relationships and one of them is in the electronic world.

THE OXYMORON OF ELECTRONIC INTIMACY

In our hectic, crowded world, it is easy to be comforted by the ease of communicating via electronics. The development of the Internet has connected the world like never before. But can these connections that people are making via e-mail and chat rooms provide the sharing that is necessary for a relationship to develop? Is there such a thing as electronic intimacy? The answer is yes, within limits.

The telephone and the Internet can provide an interactive form of electronic intimacy. Some therapists have now started using e-mail to do therapy. It can be very helpful. For starters, it lets both the client and therapist write their concerns and responses when it is convenient for them, or at distances that might otherwise make therapy impossible. E-therapists have also discovered that people can often go more deeply into their inner psychic landscape when they don't have to deal with the physical presence of a therapist. It is like intensive journaling, where the journal talks back to you. As a result, the client can bring forth issues that might take longer to uncover in a face-to-face encounter. The e-mail format allows for depth, since both client and counselor can carefully consider what they have to say to each other.

Chat rooms and electronic buddies also can lead to quite a candid level of personal sharing—one of the principles of increasing intimacy. The electronic version of personal sharing does create a kind of intimacy that can be quite satisfying. For many people it has opened up a whole new world.

All the benefits of e-therapy can apply to chat rooms and e-mail relationships, which is why e-romances get started so quickly. But a word of warning here. It is very easy, when we are hungry for a close, bonded relationship, to be vulnerable to hearing what we want to hear. It is easy to fall into a fantasy of romance that clouds our judgment. A true long-term, bonded relationship lives and breathes on the foundation of commitment. That commitment can be pretty thin over the wire. Eventually you will have to step away from the computer or the telephone and develop a face-to-face contact if you want an e-relationship to mature fully.

I must confess that I have a bias. For over a million years, community has happened mostly in the olfactory zone. When people were close enough to smell each other, they were close enough for community. Real human contact happens when we can smell the fragrance of cooking, perfume, breath, and sweat. It is in close physical proximity where limbic resonance really comes alive. Of course, lots of community happens outside of the olfactory zone, but not much of anything intimate. Electronic communities will remain on the low end of the intimacy scale if the people involved never find their way into the same room.

For people who are uncomfortable with intimacy, electronic connections are a great way to be with others. Teenagers, who are still learning the skills of intimacy, will spend hours on the phone, a more traditional form of electronic communication. When they are face to face, they have too much data to process. Smell, non-verbal clues, facial expressions, and the demand for a more immediate response are all required. For a young person still mastering this complex interaction, it is more comfortable to be on the phone where she has to deal only with words and voice tone. In time she will learn other skills and no longer need that buffer.

But again, a cautionary note is needed. This buffer can sometimes prevent you from taking the full measure of the person with whom you are interacting. Some people have personality disturbances or are dangerous predators who can hide easily behind a silver tongue. They can be very clever in saying exactly what you want to hear, and leave you feeling like you have found your soulmate. When you are not face to face, these people can easily fool you because you do not have the other clues that would normally tip you off to be careful. And since the e-relationship is so private, it lacks the balancing presence of your personal village—of others looking over your shoulders to warn you when something is not right. It is easy for a stranger who is up to no good to lure an unsuspecting person, who is assuming goodwill, into something dangerous.

Research shows very clearly that most people report a lower sense of belonging with electronic communities and relationships than in face-to-face contact. These instant connections may be exciting, a chance to establish contact and even to begin to develop friendships, but they are not enough. Research suggests that the closer we are to the olfactory zone, the greater the sense of belonging.

You Can Dial Up The Level Of Intimacy You Want

We have seen how personal intimacy is increased when people spend more time together and share their lives with each other. Close face-to-face contact increases intimacy. But true intimacy takes a large commitment of time and energy to develop and maintain, and none of us have unlimited time and energy. As a result, most of the people who make up the fabric of our personal villages are affiliates: those with whom we share some common ground but do not share much about our inner lives.

A well-balanced personal village will contain a spectrum from one end of the intimacy continuum to the other. Of course the amount of intimacy you want depends to a large degree on your personal preference. Each of us is different and comfortable with differing kinds of intimacy. Take care of yourself and find the level that works for you. Too little intimacy can lead to alienation. Too much can overwhelm you and lead to a loss of time to be with yourself. Create a balance. You will have to do this yourself because no one else will do it for you. No one can.

OBSERVE THE VIRTUES

Kindness.
The very nature of kindness is to spread.
If you are kind to others,
Today they will be kind to you,
And tomorrow to someone else.

Shri Chinmoy

Although most people in your personal village will fall outside of your most intimate circles, it is absolutely essential that you treat every person you encounter as if he or she were a great being. It's true. Each person you meet, from your most intimate friend to your most casual contact, the guy in line next to you at the hamburger stand, deserves to be treated with great kindness and respect. Great thinkers have always advised us to observe the classic virtues. They are not new. Everyone has heard them.

THE VIRTUES

- *Be courteous and kind to every person you meet.*
- *Walk through your world with charity and goodwill.*
- *Hold compassion and empathy for every person.*
- *Be generous with your resources.*
- *Practice respect in every encounter.*

Some of you will protest that you do not want to be kind in a world filled with rude and obnoxious people who make life difficult. You're right, there are many unpleasant people, and some people are the source of much evil and pain. So why should you be nice to them? You cannot please everyone or be pleasing to everyone. The answer is simple: It's not about them, it's about you. When you are respectful to others, you bring respect into your life and it begins to glow around you. You will begin to feel it, and others will too. In time, your respectfulness and graciousness will become contagious and begin to infect those around you. Kindness is one way each of us can change the small world around us and have a positive impact on those in our personal village.

True intimacy will nourish the deepest place inside of you. It is a refuge from an over-pressurized world. It keeps you in balance as you seek to traverse the journey from birth to death with dignity and meaning. Creating and maintaining intimacy is not easy, but for those few with whom you achieve the degree of intimacy you want, it is worth the effort.

You might start an epidemic of goodwill with your kindness.

By understanding the intimacy continuum, you can adjust the degree of intimacy you want and stay connected to all levels of your vital personal village. In the next few chapters, I'll take you from the least intimate—the informal place of the promenade and your neighborhood—to the most intimate. Let's start with the large sea of people who surround you and roam around in your network.

In Summary

- We need to be entrained with each other to keep our body chemistry in balance. That is why we are community animals.

- Robert Heinlein coined the term grok, meaning to know another so well that it is as if his or her inner experience is your own.

- The ability to be intimate grows out of years of interacting with many people.

- Intimacy varies along the continuum of human relationships.

- Virtues strengthen our relationships along the whole spectrum of intimacy.

    - Be courteous and kind to every person you meet.
    - Walk through your world with charity and goodwill.
    - Hold compassion and empathy with each encounter.
    - Be generous with your resources.
    - Practice respect with each meeting.

- Diversify across the whole spectrum of intimacy.

- Context is an important influence on whether intimacy happens.

- True intimacy comes only with honest, mutual, personal sharing.

- True intimacy takes time and effort.

- Electronic intimacy does exist, but within limits.

- When you know the continuum, you can dial up the degree of intimacy you want and need.

Resources You Can Use

Stranger in a Strange Land by Robert Heinlein, 1961

> The word grok first found its way into our language through this story. If you like good science fiction and have never read this story, it is a good tale with a subtle message.

The Dance of Intimacy by Harriet Lerner, 1989

> This wonderful book was originally written for women during the heyday of feminism. It is full of heart, wisdom, and practical ideas about how to be in an intimate relationship.

A General Theory of Love by Thomas Lewis, M.D., Fari Amini, M.D., and Richard Lannon, M.D., 2000

> This short little book is a definitive synthesis of everything scientists have learned about how the brain contributes to that universal and impossible-to-define experience we call love. It is a must-read for policy makers, psychologists, psychotherapy clients, parents with little children, and everyone who wants to know the real story about love and human relationships.

The Art of Intimacy by Thomas Malone, M.D., and Patrick Malone, M.D., 1987

> Many books have been written about intimacy, but this classic says it all. It is intellectual and will appeal to those who want to know the real underpinnings of intimacy.

Passionate Marriage by David Schnarch, Ph.D., 1997

> This is the book to read about the dance between knowing yourself and being intimate with another. It is a rich resource for anyone in an intimate relationship. I recommend it highly.

The Anatomy of Love by Helen Fisher, 1992

> If you want a fascinating tour through the history and chemistry of relationships and the reasons for their complex twists and turns, this is a great read.

You've Got Mail, a film starring Tom Hanks and Meg Ryan, 1999

> A delightful, light romantic comedy that highlights the dimensions of electronic intimacy and shows that true intimacy only occurs when the people involved finally come into each other's physical presence.

CHAPTER 4

Roaming In Your Personal Village

Roaming is an ancient human activity, as old as our evolutionary roots. People gather in many places: homes, work, the community commons, and in the electronic world. We make emotional attachments to the places where we habitually roam and the people we meet there. Three simple strategies for roaming and developing new relationships are 1) keep showing up, 2) wander around, and 3) hang out. When we roam in our physical world and among the people who inhabit it, we personally reap a rich harvest for our lives, and we enrich and uplift the lives of those we touch.

Roaming is as old as human experience. For three million years we evolved while living a hunter-gatherer lifestyle. By the time our species, Homo sapiens, came along, we had progressed to hunter-collectors because we roamed our countryside and collected useful items to bring back to our little bands. We searched and roamed and collected over so many millions of years that countless numbers of circuits evolved in our brains to support our wanderings.

Even though we no longer call ourselves roaming hunter-collectors, we still are. If you want to see hunter-collector activity in action, go to the local mall, grocery store, beach, or hardware store.

Scores of people are roaming and searching for treasures to take home. Some won't even use what they gather, they will simply collect and store what they find.

I remember asking my eccentric friend Richard why he saved 5,000 empty tuna fish cans. He replied, "I have no idea. I just couldn't bear to throw away so many of the same thing." As we talked, we were standing in the middle of his crowded basement, piled to the ceiling with treasures he had collected from years of prowling in surplus stores. These were treasures for which he had no use, but he could not resist bringing them home. His hunter-collector brain was still at work, though instead of roots and berries and a stone tool he collected lathes, old searchlights, and tuna fish cans. You know people like this. Their cupboards are full of useful things they may never use.

In today's language we call people who do this hoarders or pack rats or obsessive compulsives. But in fact it is not so strange that all of us roam and search for treasures because we evolved genetically to do just that. And as we roam, search, hunt, and collect, we find the treasures that support our lives.

In our efforts to collect, we roam throughout our territory. Not only do we roam in our physical world but we also roam in our people world. Your personal village contains everything you will ever need as you negotiate the grand journey from birth to death. So use your ancient brain to go searching in your community. It will serve you well. Roaming through the village of people around us is one of the great adventures of life.

GET PERSONAL AND WANDER AROUND

Our new gadgets provide us with an efficiency in connecting to others that is a great boon, but eventually we have to get up close and personal if we are to have any more than superficial contact.

Once while visiting my parents I asked my mother where Dad was. "Oh, probably down the alley talking to the neighbors," was her reply. And indeed he was. I found him with a teenager under the hood of a car. Before long the car was lurching down the alley in a cloud of smoke, so I joined Dad as he continued his rounds until he discovered Lois on her back porch. Another half hour followed, chatting about arthritis, grandchildren, and the weather. So it went for two hours until we arrived back home for afternoon coffee.

Jake, a neighbor, was already there. He had stopped by to report on the auction up at Springdale. Mom had coffee and cake ready for the inevitable afternoon crowd. My sister and her children stopped by to see if they needed anything from the store. The Bomsteads dropped in. A little more coffee, lots of talk, and soon it was time for dinner.

I was participating in the ever-swirling circles of family, friends, and neighbors that were a daily part of my parents' lives. As I watched, I realized that except for the family, this collection of people was in place because my father constantly reached out to meet new people and renew old contacts with anyone who was near. He made friends simply by wandering around and making small talk with everyone he came in contact with. After a lifetime of doing this, he had accumulated a personal village that was amazingly rich and diverse. You can do this too.

You can develop a habit of chatting about little things with the people who populate your daily life. Ask the clerk in the store how the day is going. Talk with the kids down the block about their games. Speak with your neighbors about the traffic or the roses. If you live in an apartment, talk about security or the neighbors or parking. At your job, stop and chat with the person in the next workstation, as long as you do not interfere with his work. Even if you do not have any need to talk with the cleaning lady, talk with her anyway. Everyone needs human warmth and acknowledgment, and maybe she will know something from her vantage point

Wandering around and talking with everyone you encounter is the ancient way of meeting people.

-63-

that will be enlightening to you. Simply wander around and make small talk. With time and familiarity, comfort will come. When you roam in your personal village, everyone benefits.

There is actually a business strategy called "management by wandering around." The supervisor makes it a point to spend time with many of the workers to find out exactly what they are doing, what their challenges are, and what they need in order to succeed in their jobs. In one company, the CEO sometimes spends part of a day riding around with one of the truck drivers. He quickly learns the challenges these drivers face and what they need. After all, the job of a manager is to make sure that all workers are successful at their jobs. Face-to-face contact with the staff brings them closer to that goal. As a result, the job becomes more fun and satisfying for everyone and, as a by-product, productivity soars.

You can do the same thing by wandering around at school or in the dorm or in your neighborhood or in the bowling alley. Anyplace where there is a mix of people who share something in common with you is a good place to wander around. Some of these people will be receptive to your reaching out, even in very casual ways. As you do so, your net of people will keep expanding.

Remember, most of the people you meet at school, at work, or in your neighborhood will be low on the intimacy scale. They may have meaning and enrich your time in that place but, with a few exceptions, they will never become your close intimates. Talking with your teacher, sharing a joke or a bit of gossip with a fellow student, offering some useful information to a neighbor or coworker—a great recipe, a new dress shop, the name of a good mechanic—is the lubricant that makes our daily lives work smoothly. Even something as simple as a smile or holding a door open for a passing stranger lights a bright place in the world. You do yourself and everyone you meet a favor if you find a way to make some kind of actual human contact as you pass.

THE PLACES WHERE WE GATHER

We roam in many places, and each place has its own level of intimacy. Some social scientists have suggested that we divide our time between three places: First Place, Second Place, and Third Place. First Place is our home environment with our immediate family. Second Place refers to our work or school environment, and Third Place refers to those public gathering places where people meet, mingle, and find a sense of connection to the larger community. In reality this is an artificial division. But the point is that we engage with people on a continuum of intimacy and activity that includes many places. For discussion's sake, let's pretend that these three places do exist distinctly. Later we will add some more designations to fill out the picture.

FIRST PLACE

Your most intimate social interactions will usually happen within the confines of the family. You will have either a natural family or an alternative family, or maybe a combination of both. Your First Place people—spouse, children, brothers and sisters, parents and grandparents, aunts, uncles, close family friends, and confidants—are the core foundation for your life. If this place is alive and vital, it is the refuge to which you can always return at the end of a hectic day.

First Place is the intimate family circle.

When we are children these people guide us and open resources for us by getting us into good schools, by taking us to good doctors and music teachers, and by enrolling us in Tae Kwon Do. Often it is our parents or close friends of the family who help us find our first job.

When we grow up we first move into a transitional family, usually made up of fellow students or friends either living together or nearby. In time we develop our own immediate family or alternative family. Then we have a whole other host of people who expand our most intimate circle. Much more about that later.

Isabelle, widowed and crippled with arthritis, still lived in her family home, but alone. Her daughter, Ruth, was her main contact in the world. Ruth took her to the doctor and shopping and managed to spend time with her several times a week. Ruth's three children had known Grandma since they were born. The weekly contact Isabelle had with her grandchildren was the focal point of her life. Watching them grow and being a part of that experience gave her life meaning.

Isabelle's favorite granddaughter, Suzanne, experienced her grandmother as an anchor point in her life and confided in her about school and boys and her future. When Suzanne left for college, she wrote often to Grandma and sometimes called. And when she got married, Isabelle was in the front row. When Isabelle grew ill and was hospitalized, Suzanne dropped everything to fly to her side. These two women nourished the link between them until the day Suzanne stood beside her grandmother's coffin with tears of gratitude. That connection across the generations was a thread of continuity that added fullness to both of their lives.

Your family members, even the more distant ones, offer an emotional sense of roots that brings security and offers nourishment to your life. In the Jewish tradition this extended family is called your *mishpoche* (pronounced *misch-po-ka*), and it includes everyone who is related to you, from the most intimate to the most remotely distant relative. These family members can sometimes open doors that you could never pry open yourself. And you do the same for them.

Don't forget the friends of the family. I have painted a picture of an ideal family, which may not always exist. Sometimes a person who is distant or cut off from his or her own immediate family will adopt or be adopted into an intimate family. If you have some of these people in your family system, treat them with respect and kindness and remember them at important times. Though this adopted family member may be a close friend to your parents or children, do not forget that you too may be a very important person to her. She draws a sense of belonging and comfort from knowing you.

This is so important that in Japan, older, isolated people have even taken to renting a family so that they can be near the comforting warmth of children and family life. The family earns a little money by opening up their home to a forgotten or seemingly discarded older person. The older person has children to play with and buy presents for, and family celebrations and events to sustain his spirits. It may sound commercial, but the alternative can be deadly, literally.

SECOND PLACE

Everyone has a job: the mom taking care of kids; the student working at studies; the high school student babysitting younger siblings; the carpenter building houses; the accountant doing taxes. Regardless of what we do, most of us have an intense network associated with our work.

For children whose immediate family is skimpy or dysfunctional, the school environment may provide additional people to support and sustain them. Jamie's mother worked full time to support her children, living in a small apartment. Juggling childcare, her job, and home responsibilities often left Jamie's mom tired and not as available as either of them wanted. But at school Jamie found caring human contact with an understanding teacher and a circle of friends. What she had at school helped to soften the effects of her stressed family system. Her mother was relieved

> *Second Place is school or work.*

that the school offered this dimension to Jamie's life. Even when the family is strong, school can be a rich environment, providing experiences and values that complement the family.

Phyllis lives alone, and because of her intense shyness tends to be socially isolated. She struggles emotionally with the resistance inside herself to reach out and find friends. Even at church she tends to stay to herself. Though she is of retirement age, she continues to work because there she has a ready-made circle of people who nourish her. As an experienced account executive in a bank, she must interact with customers and fellow workers in a way that transcends her shyness. All the people at her job are very important to her. She remembers their birthdays, the details of their families, and their likes and dislikes. She shows up with birthday cakes and revels in stories about her coworkers' children. The people in the office are so important that she never misses a day.

We may never know how important we are to some of the people at work. It is a gift to and from the highest place in our human spirit to treat every person in our workplace with great kindness and respect.

So roam freely at work. What you will learn there will not only help you enhance your job performance but will also help you strengthen your personal relationships. Often work is where you first meet some of the most important people in your life.

THIRD PLACE

Outside of home and work, people have always gravitated toward physical places in their community where they can informally hang out with each other. Sociologists call these places the *commons*. That means they belong to everyone in common. Everyone is welcome to come and hang out and interact. Today the commons could be the mall or the sidewalk or the park. In medieval times, the commons referred to the fields that belonged to the whole village. Everyone had a share of the field in which to plant crops. All were welcome to graze their cows on the common fields. Though the house was private, the streets and fields were considered the commons and available to everyone.

Throughout time the commons has referred to the place where everyone in a particular group, family, neighborhood, or town is entitled to gather whenever they wish. The family bedroom is private, but the living room or the kitchen can be the commons for a family. The work station for an account executive may be private, but the lunchroom is the commons where any of the workers can gather or come and go at will. In effect, the commons is the place where members of a group do not have to knock to enter, and where everyone in the group is free to use the resources.

For some, the commons is the Internet. For others, it's the pub. In today's more populated world, there is comfort to be found in hanging out at a familiar place with others, even if most of the people are strangers. At least they are all listening to the same musicians or drinking the same coffee or reading the same newspapers.

Often a Third Place commons is one created by a business, like a coffee shop, bookstore, or food court. But it can also be a town square, a park, or any other place where we can walk and promenade. On the Internet these electronic commons are called chat rooms.

In Bellevue, Washington, Ron Sher, a wise community builder, incorporated an attractive Third Place into his shopping center. The public gathering place is in the very middle of the center. Ron likes to think of it as the community living room. Clustered together are coffee shops, a food court, childcare, hairdressers, public chessboards, a coin shop, and

> *Third Place is the public commons, a place where everyone is welcome to take in the noisy, welcoming crowd, or simply to sit quietly on the edge and bask in the buzz of the hive.*

a wing of City Hall. The public library has a small branch there that draws more people than any other branch in the library system. All day long people roam in this common area to meet friends, to have lunch, and to take a break from the push of the day. In the morning the mall walkers gather. Later the disabled collect to talk, compare notes, and get out of the weather. Business people have power-networking meetings at the coffee shop or in the food court. Moms with little kids in tow meet fellow moms for some adult company. In the afternoon the teenagers troop in for food and to hang out with each other. At dinnertime families show up for a quick meal in the ever-swirling circles of people. A stage has been placed on the edge of the food court, and on Friday and Saturday evenings musicians perform, drawing large informal crowds of friends and neighbors.

The shopping center does not make a direct profit from this Third Place operation, but it does bring people into the adjacent stores. The real value of this commons is that it provides a community center in an otherwise apartment-dense, automobile-dominated, pedestrian-unfriendly environment. The shopping center prospers. The community prospers.

In the commons, a sense of belonging to our fellow community members takes root.

Margaret used her knowledge of hanging around in a Third Place to improve her life. She used the hang-out strategy to combat the loneliness of widowhood after her husband of 43 years passed away. Her family and the former neighbors had moved away. She was dependent upon a phone call from her daughter for human contact. Margaret felt stranded. In her wanderings through the local shopping district, she noticed a cafe where retirees gathered every day. So she began to hang out every morning over a cup of tea and later in the day for lunch. At least for an hour a day she was with people, who were all strangers at first. In time the regulars grew to recognize her and invited her to join them. Now she had a place where she was known by name and would be missed if she didn't show up. No longer was she totally dependent for contact on the weekly phone call from her daughter in a distant city.

Bob tells how a chance interaction in a Third Place answered a deep longing. He had lived in Hawaii for several months and, in spite of considerable effort, had been unsuccessful in connecting with any locals who shared his interest in Buddhist mysticism. So he began to hang out in a little bookstore-cafe where he could read about this topic. One day a woman at the next table noticed the title of his book and joined him. He soon discovered that she had lived in Hawaii all her life and knew many of the people he wanted to meet. After a lengthy visit she invited him to attend a meeting at her house. There he found a gathering of fellow travelers.

E-PLACE

The electronic world is a marvelous place for finding and interacting with people who share your interests. So many people have begun to gather in the electronic environment that it deserves a name of its own. I call it E-Place. We tend to think of E-Place as the Internet, but remember, we have developed a love affair with the telephone over a number of decades. For many people, the telephone is the link to other people that lubricates the daily workings of their lives.

In a way, television also provides us with a simple way to keep connected with the world around us, though that medium is one way as of this writing. Television and radio connect us in real time to the events in our world. For people who are shut in or isolated, they are a window to the world.

More recently, computers have given us the ability to locate almost any person who shares our common interest with just a few simple commands. If you are geographically isolated from the people who are important to you or do not know how to find them, the electronic world will fill the need very quickly. For shut-ins and the lonely, the electronic community is a godsend.

E-place is a commons without walls where communities of people with similar interests can find each other and share ideas and resources.

Electronic connections are essential for business and professional networking. Telephones, e-mails, and chat rooms are good for enhancing our relationships. They allow us to maintain more frequent contact, which in turn strengthens our connection. But do remember that electronic connections often tend to be single-stranded. Single-stranded means that two people have a relationship with each other as a solo pair, with no other connections to others whom they both know. E-Places are a good starting point and an excellent way to maintain contact, sometimes quite intense, with a broad community of people. We need many single-stranded connections to maintain variety, but if we do not balance our personal village with multi-stranded relationships as we roam, our lives can get out of balance. Chat rooms and conference calls are multi-stranded, but more about that later.

INFORMAL PLACE

Social scientists describe First, Second, and Third Place, but in reality this is a simplified way of describing where people roam and interact. We actually interact in many different places for which we have no labels. One of these public places is what I call Informal Place. Informal Place encompasses everything outside of First, Second, Third, and E-Place. Informal Place is your neighborhood: it's grocery stores, bus stops, and back alleys; the list is endless.

> *Informal Places are all the places between First, Second, Third, and E-Place where we find people.*

An example of Informal Place is the promenade, a commons with no commercial focus to which people flock. Most cities have a promenade where people gather to walk, strut, and look at each other. In many Southern European town squares, the entire population comes out every evening to walk back and forth. People stop to talk and take different people by the arm for the short stroll. This promenade goes on every evening for a couple of hours. It is our nature to promenade. Teenagers have known this for a long time, as they strut in front of each other or go cruising down the strip to see and be seen.

Our hunter-collector brains will keep us searching through all the nooks and crannies of the places in our world. Even outside of formal gathering places, we will continue to find treasures and people. Roaming everyplace where people are found and talking with those we meet will sometimes turn up surprising information and resources, nice additions that add spice and life to our own personal village.

ANCHORING

When you have a good time roaming in your familiar haunts—the fabric shop, park, cafe, or school—that good feeling becomes anchored to those places and you will feel nourished whenever you go back there. Anchoring is the basis for a sense of belonging. Anchoring is part of our human nature. It is a psychological term that describes our tendency to become emotionally attached to a place, an event, or a physical sensation. We go back to that which is familiar because it makes us comfortable and at ease. It is our way of remembering the good things we would like to repeat and the bad things we want to avoid.

Having a great time with a friend in a restaurant will anchor us to the restaurant. When we go back to the restaurant, we feel good. We will want to go back to that friend and that restaurant, and maybe even to the same table. This is called a positive anchor. Of course if you have a dreadful experience someplace, you can develop a negative anchor. Then anytime you think about or go to that place you will become anxious and uncomfortable, and you may even have panic attacks.

> *Anchoring is the basis for a sense of belonging.*

ROAMING

Sherry talks about when she lived in a high-rise in New York City. Each day she would go for walks on the street, talking with doormen, street people, and shop owners. She knew them all by name, and they knew her. None of them knew that she was a world-renowned psychologist, but they did know that she lived nearby. She tells how Horst, who ran the butcher shop around the corner, was one of her favorites. Every day she dropped in to look over Horst's selections of meats. And every day Horst told her what she was going to have for dinner that night. Sherry felt known and somehow loved by Horst's control over her diet. Every afternoon she would take the elevator down to the street and wonder what he had for her that day. After Horst had defined her evening's meal, she talked with Natalie at the produce stand, bought a paper from Louie who had all the neighborhood news, and then picked out flowers at Sasha's stall. Every day Sherry roamed in her neighborhood. Roaming in the middle of that familiar cast of neighbors gave her life fullness and belonging. In her private life she had her friends, colleagues, and family members. But her anchor to the people and scenes on the street, and all the brief interactions that were included, was a garnish that gave fuller meaning to being a New Yorker.

Roaming does take effort. Even if you're a natural, it helps to have a strategy. I will introduce you to three, which we will talk about next.

Three Strategies for Roaming in Your Personal Village
1. *Wander around and hang out.*
2. *Make many brief appearances and keep showing up.*
3. *Apply the Principle of Seven.*

WANDER AROUND AND HANG OUT
This is what my father did to build his strong circle of associates and friends. This ancient way has worked for a million years. Each of you has a natural territory in which you roam. Maybe it is your work place or the neighborhood or a haunt where you have a positive anchor and a place where you feel comfortable. It could be a cafe at the market, your church, or your neighborhood. It could be any of the many places where you roam to collect treasures.

Research shows that relationships tend to build between people who inhabit the same places. It's simple. Just put yourself in a location where others are doing the same thing as you, then wander around and hang out. That is what Margaret did when she purposely hung out in the cafe with other seniors, and that is what Bob did when he began to hang out in the bookstore-cafe in Hawaii.

Jack used the same idea. Jack was wheelchair-bound with cerebral palsy. Wherever he went, people gave him a wide berth because he looked, talked, and moved awkwardly. It was very difficult for him to make friends. His attendant suggested he try hanging out in a nearby meditation center. It was not easy because even though the people there were superficially friendly, they too were uncomfortable with his awkward way of moving and of talking. But Jack was persistent and applied the two additional strategies for roaming that I will talk about next: make continued, brief appearances and keep showing up. Probably some of the members of the center wished he would go away because his presence made them uncomfortable, but Jack did not stop showing up for meditation programs, and he hung around during the following fellowship time. After a while, a few people made the effort to talk with him, and eventually he came to be accepted as one of the regulars.

MAKE MANY BRIEF APPEARANCES AND KEEP SHOWING UP

This strategy follows naturally from hanging out. By nature people want to engage, but they are cautious. From past experience, we all know there are individuals who will invade our space, take advantage of us, or hurt us emotionally. In addition, almost all of us have a hidden, inner belief that we are inadequate or that there is something wrong with us. The risk of being invaded or hurt once again, or of having that universal inner belief that we are inadequate be exposed, causes most people to be initially on guard. We tend to proceed into new relationships with caution, as a natural way of guarding ourselves against hurt. By applying the strategy of making many brief contacts—on the turf of the person you'd like to know and appropriate to the common ground—trust and comfort can develop in a way that is natural for both of you.

THE PRINCIPLE OF SEVEN

There is actually a scientific basis for hanging out and making brief appearances. Studies have defined how many contacts must occur before comfort can develop between new people. According to Harvard psychologist Dr. George Miller, the average human mind will keep track of a number of events up to about seven. The number of events is fewer for some and greater for others, but for most people it is about seven. After approximately seven events, the brain will make an internal accounting shift and lump them all into the category of *many*. The mind simply stops counting after a while, and most people experience this internal shift as "familiar." With this shift to familiarity also comes increased comfort.

After the seventh contact or so, the internal shift to familiarity occurs. It is almost like the brain says, "Oh, she has been around for a while. She's an okay person." At that point you shift from the status of outsider to insider. Everything gets easier.

After seven appearances, people will begin to consider you an insider.

Professionals use this method to build a network of colleagues and potential business contacts. Mediators use this technique to slowly build up trust and familiarity for resolving conflicts and negotiating contracts. Sales representatives use the Principle of Seven to build trust as a base for more fruitful business relationships.

Repeated brief contacts work. The professionals make it work for them, and you can make it work for you. Erik did.

Erik described for me how he purposefully went about meeting a woman in his apartment building. For months he established familiarity by simply saying "Hello" when they passed in the hall. Then one day she left her car lights on. A knock on her door earned a hurried thank you, as she scurried away to turn off the lights. Two months later they encountered each other in the laundry room, where they exchanged small talk about the weather. He knew she sometimes went to the storage lockers on Saturday morning to get her bicycle, so he began organizing his locker at those times. One morning she showed up and noticed his scuba gear. She was curious and stopped to talk. They were getting acquainted through all these "chance" encounters.

After many months, Erik knew he was interested and decided the time was ripe to see if she was too. He went to her apartment and asked if she had any quarters for the washing machine, even though he had a pocket full of quarters. A week later he dropped by to borrow a cup of flour for pancakes. The following day she showed up to borrow some lemons. This time she stayed, and they talked more about diving and about their work and their families. The following Sunday he invited her for breakfast. She accepted.

From there it was easy to learn that she was interested in pursuing the relationship. His patient efforts over several months had paid off with a sense of familiarity and safety. He had conveyed to her the attitude that he would respect her boundaries and not hurry her, and that he was consistent. He succeeded in becoming one of the insiders in her world. He had also given her signals that he was interested in getting to know her better. This was many years ago. His patience paid off. Today they are married and have two children.

Erik's approach may seem a bit old-fashioned to some. Many people are in such a rush to find contact that they do not take this much time, yet this style is preferable. I often see people who married after a very brief courtship, only to discover later that they did not share any common ground beyond the initial attraction. They rushed into total commitment, only to find total disappointment. The chance of a relationship developing some staying power is much better with Erik's patient, methodical approach. ·

A series of brief encounters where two people have a chance to watch each other in action over time is a powerful tool in building trust and mutual comfort. Brief repeated contacts provide the mechanism behind the strategies of hanging out and wandering around that we talked about earlier.

There are some basic rules of behavior that will help to make your roaming more effective. Susan Roane is a professional networker and author. She advises frequent contacts when developing relationships, and encourages people to roam in their people circles in very much the same way that I have been talking about. Here is a condensed version of her advice.

Roaming Effectively

- *Treat people with respect, courtesy, and honesty.*
- *Do what you say you are going to do.*
- *Listen with your ears, eyes, head, and heart.*
- *Reach out to others when you do not need anything in return from them.*
- *Treat people as unique beings with lives and hearts, not as contacts on your list.*
- *Be liberal with your praise, and pass that praise on to others.*
- *Express your thanks for all the gifts you have received from others.*
- *Do good deeds for others.*
- *Have fun and laugh a lot.*

As you can see, roaming in your personal village can lead to a wide range of relationships, from the least intimate to the most intimate. Roaming is the place to start when people do not present themselves naturally in your life. Even if you have a good circle of close people already, you will enrich your life by roaming around like our hunter-collector ancestors. Find out what is in your surrounding world. The treasures you will unearth will be surprising.

The next step on our journey from least intimate to most intimate is that collection of people with whom you have something
in common—anything. I call these folks your neighbors. So far we
have been talking about how to roam among strangers who can
become known to you. Another group of people who are important
are neighbors, people who happen to live or work close to where
you find yourself. Developing relationships with them is more than
just random roaming, and though it requires all the things mentioned here, there is more. Let's turn our attention to developing
relationships with our neighbors.

IN SUMMARY

- You will find people in every setting where you spend time: First Place, Second Place, Third Place, E-Place, and Informal Place.

- Be persistent and purposeful about roaming in your personal village.

- Wander around and make small talk with anyone who is receptive.

- Find a hangout and become a regular.

- Initially, make many brief appearances to develop familiarity.

- Keep showing up.

- Be as curious in your exploration as our hunter-collector ancestors.

- The Principle of Seven is the science for establishing familiarity.

RESOURCES YOU CAN USE

Great Good Places by Ray Oldenberg, 1997

This is a magnificent book describing the many places where people gather in the commons. If you are interested in reading an in-depth study of Third Place dynamics, this is the book for you.

Bathing in Public in the Roman World by Garrett G. Fagan, 1999

The public baths in old Rome were the public living rooms of that society. People gathered to talk, network, play, relax, and wash. The baths were an important daily event of Roman life—the Starbucks of 2000 years ago. If you are a Third Place theorist, this academic work is a great reference.

How to Win Friends and Influence People by Dale Carnegie, 1937

Yes, you saw it right: 1937. Dale Carnegie's first version of his famous classic is a jewel about how to form relationships and take care of them. It was such a hit that a whole institute grew up around the idea. Since then several editions, written by professional writers and seminar leaders, have been released under the same name. The ideas he developed are well worth studying. But if you want a treat, find an original 1937 version in a used bookstore. It will delight you.

Finding Forrester, a film starring Rob Brown and Sean Connery, 2001

> If you want to see how the Principle of Seven works, watch this film. It is the story of a young student, Jamal, and an old recluse who reach back and forth to each other and succeeded in creating a significant mentor-student relationship after seven contacts. And later in the film a girl uses the Principle of Seven to develop a meaningful relationship with Jamal. It is a well-made film and a beautiful story of relationships and the challenges of life.

Door to Door, a film starring William Macy and Kyra Sedgwick, 2002

> Inspired by the true life story of Bill Porter, this film shows a man with cerebral palsy who, in his determination to be a salesman, keeps showing up, uses brief contacts and persistence, and practices the virtues. In the end he becomes an institution who transforms a neighborhood. It is an inspiring and touching story about a man who impacted the lives of everyone he met.

CHAPTER 5

Rubbing Elbows With Your Neighbors

Your neighbors are the people with whom you roam in your personal village and with whom you share common ground. To interact with them nourishes your soul and adds value to your neighborhood. Evidence shows that when people take part in public events, like attending church or going to ball games, they are happier and live longer. The interaction of neighbors with each other can be a powerful catalyst for positive change and a critical element in maintaining the quality of the entire community. When we meet in the commons of our neighborhood, we have a natural license to interact. When we interact with a generous heart and treat every person with respect, the entire society benefits.

What a commotion! I was standing on a ladder ten feet above a throng of babbling, happy, expectant runners, all waiting for the starting signal to mark the beginning of The Race for the Cure. This crowd of 10,000 men and women had gathered for a run to support the defeat of breast cancer. Those who had personally triumphed over breast cancer wore pink shirts and hats. Many wore a pink placard with the name of a woman or a man who had died of this disease. There was a sea of pink hats and placards. From my perch I watched a young man with three children in tow thread his way through the crowd—all four wearing pink placards bearing the name of the same woman. Everyone was friendly and excited and eager to take part in this very important event.

I had lugged my heavy ladder and camera gear over a mile to photograph this gathering. Tired and feeling a little trepidation, I set my ladder up in the exact middle of the milling crowd and began taking pictures. The high platform of the ladder was a perfect place to shoot pictures, and it was also the only place to get above the crowd to spot a friend. So every few minutes I would feel a tug on my pant leg as someone asked to climb up to look for a companion. My presence as a photographer in their midst had become part of their experience.

Everyone was eager to talk and share their stories. All of them were vibrant and bright and grateful to be alive, and very generous with their warm smiles. Yet many participants' eyes reflected a subtle soberness that spoke of lessons learned about the fragility and preciousness of life. As the beginning of the race neared, I pulled my ladder back and continued shooting as all 10,000 of them raced off in a floodtide of love and remembrance. Tears filled my eyes and my chest was heavy. Standing on my ladder, I sobbed as I watched the bobbing crowd flow away from me. I was surprised at the intensity of my reaction.

> *A crowd creates its own energy.*

Yet the powerful energy generated by this large assembly of people also felt familiar. Be it the excitement of a game, the giddy happiness of a parade, the thrill of attending a concert, or the sadness of a funeral, we have all felt that unique bond while in the midst of a group gathered for a common purpose. I felt enveloped by the company of my neighbors, and that company touched and nourished my soul.

WHO ARE YOUR NEIGHBORS?

What makes up your neighborhood? Is it the city? Is it the Internet? Is it the mall or the folks next door? Is it the park? Is it a parade or a ball game or the opera? Is it The Race for the Cure? Yes!

Your neighbors are all the people with whom you roam, literally or virtually. They are the people who share a common place or interest with you, but for the most part they are total strangers. A few will be familiar strangers—people you recognize but do not know their names or very much about them—like the lady at the bus stop you see every morning. Some of them you know a little better, like the barista at the espresso cart, and some you know even better, like the family next door.

> *Think of the neighborhood as the forest and fields and sunshine surrounding the greenhouse of your personal village.*

Think of the neighborhood as the forest and fields and sunshine surrounding the greenhouse of your personal village. Without that surrounding fertile ground, your greenhouse would be an isolated outpost in the desert. Out of your neighborhood comes all of the resources you will ever need to make your life and personal village work. Having a vital relationship with your neighborhood is essential to you and to everyone who is important to you.

RUBBING ANTENNA

Walter is a beekeeper. He can calmly take the lid off a hive and pull out a frame of honeycomb covered with bees. As long as he stays perfectly calm, he can watch the bees on the comb wander around in what seems to be an aimless way. Surrounded by the steady low buzz, he can join the bees as they hang out, build honeycomb, tend their young, and simply be together in a hum of bee consciousness.

Human interactions in a communal setting, such as in a commons or at a promenade, can seem aimless at first too, until one takes a moment to observe the hum of purposeful activity that is actually taking place. In the center of Trondheim, Norway, is a pedestrian-only town square. Every Saturday the entire town turns out to go shopping. The Salvation Army Band shows up to play while people wander in and out of the shops to nod and smile and visit and gossip. The young people gather in the square to play the mating game. In the local grocery store just around the corner, people greet each other and lean on their carts, visiting. A simple trip to buy groceries is a two-hour affair. Like the bees in the hive, everyone comes out to rub antennae and renew their connection with each other.

Most cities and towns have formal and informal promenades where people can walk and run for exercise, take a breath of fresh air, imbibe nature, see and be seen by their neighbors, and interact casually with strangers and acquaintances alike.

Green Lake is a jewel in the middle of Seattle, Washington. One hundred years ago, the original city planners set it aside as a park. Today at all hours, people walk and run the three miles it takes to circle the lake. They breathe in the fresh air, bask in the constantly changing light, watch young bikini-clad bodies and big-bellied men and mothers pushing strollers. Friends meet friends to talk and walk.

Ben was walking around Green Lake with a friend one day when a strange man wearing a huge smile walked up and gave him a huge bear hug. Startled, Ben pulled back in surprise. "Who are you?" he blurted out.

"Gary Stewart," was the laughing reply. "It has been a long time."

"Oh, Gary!" exclaimed Ben, and just then his eye caught sight of the pretty woman standing behind Gary with an expectant smile spread across her face.

"And Lois too!" Ben exclaimed as she joined the big hug. So as the promenade continued to flow by, this surprise reunion led into a long conversation between old friends separated by decades.

Every minute along the promenade at Green Lake, Central Park in New York City, or the Zentrum (a huge pedestrian-only core in the center of Bonn, Germany) similar experiences happen again and again.

In ancient Iran, grand structures were built to shelter the bazaar from the searing sun. Areas like these are some of the commons in Iran. You can still roam the grand bazaar in Isfahan. Originally begun 1300 years ago, it took 900 years to build and it still stands in all it magnificent architectural glory. For 1300 years people have visited, drunk coffee, shopped, and promenaded in this grand pavilion. Today you will still find the shoemaker who has a pot of water simmering in front of his stall just as his counterpart did a thousand years ago. He will stop his work, pour you a cup of tea, and visit for an hour. In the ever-swirling crowd we know others, and by knowing others and being known, we know and define ourselves.

Roaming in the commons of your community is good for you and everyone else.

In Sweden, researchers discovered that people lived longer if they regularly attended the movies, opera, or local sporting events. The researchers speculated that participation in these activities somehow stimulated the immune system. That may be true, but I think something more psychological is also going on.

When we are in the company of others, sharing in the excitement of the event, we experience a confirmation that strengthens our basic sense of self. After all, when we all cheer the excitement inside of us is mirrored by those around us, which creates a feedback loop of confirmation of our own excitement. In a subtle way we come to believe in ourselves a little more as others show evidence of sharing our experience. The internal, psychological confirmation generates a sense of well-being that probably does stimulate the immune system. Being a baseball fan or a movie buff is actually good for you. Of course you can watch baseball or movies alone at home, but I doubt that it is as beneficial as being in a live crowd.

Joining in the crowd is a powerful experience and well worth the effort. Just imagine being the only person at the symphony or the ball game. It would not be the same. Like bees, we enjoy interacting with our own kind even if we do not know anything about them personally. I strongly encourage you to go out and join your neighbors. It will be good for you and it will be good for your neighbors to have your company. Hanging out in the commons is your license to interact. Everyone there rotates around roughly the same center, so you have a natural right to walk up to anyone and engage others who share the experience. If you are at a parade, it is perfectly natural to talk with anyone about the clowns and the floats. From there your conversation can evolve to other topics of common interest. More about that in later chapters. If you are walking down your street, you are entitled to engage your neighbors about issues like the flowers or the kids or the condition of your roofs. Your conversation could lead into a polite discussion about each other's health or that of the kids, and from there it can become as intimate as seems natural.

THE ACTIVITY-CENTERED NEIGHBORHOOD EVENT

The commons or promenade, with their formal and informal aspects, are only two forms of roaming in your neighborhood. Another dimension of interaction is when you join your neighbors in some kind of event where your energy is focused together in a common purpose. This kind of activity can be either organized or spontaneous.

People join together during emergencies. When a flood threatens a town, everyone turns out to fill sandbags and brace the levy. After the September 11, 2001, tragedy in New York, when terrorists brought down the World Trade Center, strangers from all around the country, and even from around the world, converged to lend a hand.

When something is out of balance, neighbors often gather to protest. During the oppressive regime of Slobodan Milosevic in Serbia, the inhabitants of Belgrade took to the streets day after day in a huge mob to express their displeasure at the government. They danced and blew whistles and rang bells. One Christmas Eve the despised leader Milosevic tried to speak to the crowd, which responded with sarcastic chants of "We love you." Eventually the Milosevic government fell, partly because of the energy of the nationwide neighborhood. The shared energy of neighbors can be a powerful force for good.

> *There is power in a united neighborhood.*

We rub elbows with our neighbors when we lend our energy to a neighborhood coalition devoted to stopping crime or blocking an unseemly development that will degrade the place where we live. We rub elbows when we exercise in the health club or at an aerobics class. We rub elbows when we work together to clean up a vacant lot or join to help paint the home of an elderly person down the street.

You will enrich your life personally and the lives of those around you when you make the effort to join the activities going on in your neighborhood. I encourage you to take part in your neighborhood, community, or city by donating blood, taking your turn in the jury box, volunteering to tutor a student, working in a food bank, or simply picking up trash on your street. By lending energy to your community, you benefit the place where you live, contribute to the quality of life of your neighbors, and ultimately enrich your own life.

Generosity And Service

You will benefit from the contributions of time and energy that you make to your community. It's not always easy to participate, however. The neighborhood is not there simply to make your life easy or fun. It takes energy to keep it alive and healthy. Each of us has a responsibility to serve our community in a way that makes sense to us. Many people have stingy hearts, so they take what others provide and do not return anything in kind. It is imperative that we have generous hearts, not only with our close loved ones but also with everyone we meet. If you neglect your neighborhood, you neglect your personal village. Service flows out of a generous heart.

Jean decided she wanted to make an effort to meet her neighbors and improve the quality of life on her block at the same time. Because she lives in earthquake country, the city has a program to train the neighbors how to become a self-sufficient team for several days in the event of a major debilitating quake. She talked with the couple next door to see if they were interested. They were. Then she called the city and started the ball rolling. That meant she had to gather thirty families to sign up for the four-hour class. Her leadership helped weave together an entire four-block area into a focused self-help team with the skills and resources necessary to deal with a natural crisis. As a result of her stepping forward to pull this event together, she created a rich resource of people for herself and for the entire neighborhood.

> *We each have a responsibility to care for our neighbors.*

After Suzanne had her stroke it was very difficult for her to get out to the grocery store. She had to call a taxi and then use her walker as she shuffled around the store. One day while Mary Lou was walking her dog in the neighborhood, she stopped to talk with Suzanne, who was leaning over her walker trimming roses. Mary Lou soon realized that Suzanne needed help and offered to take her to the grocery store. From then on, until Suzanne went into a nursing home, Mary Lou picked her up every Saturday to go for groceries. That simple act of kindness was a boon to both the women.

Sally and Jim opened an account in a new bank. Natalie was the account manager who helped them, and later she was a great help in negotiating a loan for them. Every time they were in the bank, they noticed how besieged she was with customers. Natalie was always smiling but she did not seem to have a moment to catch her breath. Jim suggested they find a way to express their gratitude for all she had done on their behalf and to say they recognized how hard she worked. Sally hit on the idea of a big bouquet of roses at Christmas. So one day Natalie returned, tired and overwhelmed from another managers' meeting, to find two dozen roses on her desk with a simple note saying, "Thank you." A generous heart had struck again.

Maybe you can think of a way to be a generous heart in your neighborhood.

EVERY PERSON YOU MEET IS PRECIOUS

A retirement stint in the Peace Corp in Botswana taught Barbara a newfound appreciation for the depth of humanity in every single individual she encounters. She always asks the bank tellers and the checkout clerks how their shift is going. That usually leads to a more involved discussion about their day, their headache, or their sore feet. When Barbara walks away, she always says with a twinkle in her eye, "No cranky customers for you today."

It is an amazing experience to walk through the grocery store with her. She will stop and talk with moms about their babies, ask other shoppers about food choices, and chat with the workers stocking shelves, asking how their day is going. Sometimes her conversations turn into long discussions. Once I watched her in the checkout line. In front of us were two rather scruffy-looking guys with a large selection of meats, vegetables, and condiments. Barbara commented, "That looks like a feast." One of the guys was quite shy and looked away, but the other lit up to say they were going to make a stew for a shut-in lady they knew. That led into a lively conversation about the lady, their relationship with her, how they were looking after her, and their delight in cooking. Just listening to the conversation warmed my insides. Even the shy fellow offered his bit. We all went away feeling enriched by the chance interaction.

Barbara says she always makes it a point to talk with the children playing in the street. She has gotten to know quite a bit about her immediate neighbors by applying the lesson she learned in Africa to engage each person. Even though many of the people she lived with in Africa faced the tragedies of AIDS, illness, and hunger, they always welcomed each other with kindness and great respect.

Psychologist Irving Polster claimed that every person's life is so rich that you could write an entire novel about it. In fact, he wrote a book titled *Every Person's Life Is Worth a Novel.* When you stop and acknowledge the truth of another person's humanity and a little about the complexity of her life, it is a gift both to her and to you. We do not have the time or energy to have an intimate relationship with very many people, but we can treat every person we meet with civility and kindness, acknowledging our recognition that he or she has a life outside of being a clerk or a homeless street person or an anonymous stranger waiting for the bus.

> *Every person's life is worth a novel.*

When you roam in your neighborhood, you become anchored to the streets and shops and commons and the people who traffic there. This anchoring leads to a sense of familiarity and ownership, belonging and comfort. The result is that your wanderings contribute to a sense of well-being. Research shows that when we cuddle or do aerobic exercise, we release a beneficial hormone called endorphin. Maybe going to the promenade or the parade or the mall activates endorphins—who knows? The Swedish researchers I mentioned earlier suggest that this may be one reason why we benefit from each other's company.

In our walk-around-communities—our neighborhoods—we have the opportunity to serve others in both formal and informal ways. We draw social capital from the people we interact with, and we give social capital back. When the interaction in the neighborhood is strong and vital, crime decreases, teenagers have a place to belong instead of feeling like aliens, and our sense of belonging increases. As we roam, our neighborhood becomes our own. And we tend to take care of what we own. When we stay engaged with the people around us, our neighborhood is strengthened. A society with vital neighborhoods is strong. A strong society fosters a government that supports that strength. In a way, we all have a responsibility to our society to roam generously in our neighborhoods. When you treat the clerk in the drugstore with courtesy and kindness, you are adding to the social capital of the entire society.

If we believe the futurists, intelligent robots will eventually run our world. Machines will take over. Even if this unlikely event does happen, people will still go out and promenade and march in crowds and gather to attend celebrations and go on pilgrimages. Our sense of belonging and our roots are with people. It is in our genetic makeup to rub elbows with our neighbors. Machines will never replace that.

> *Your neighborhood is the fertile soil out of which community grows. Till it carefully and fully.*

As you roam in your neighborhood, you will keep finding fertile oases of people, called fellowships. These gatherings come in all forms, from the most formal to quite informal. You will find in these fellowships a sense of belonging, great meaning for yourself; and you will find many of the people who will be important in your personal village. You will want to explore some of these oases because they hold great social capital for you. Now we will turn our attention to developing the art of finding and becoming involved in a fellowship that will be just right for you.

IN SUMMARY

- The company of our neighbors nourishes our souls.

- Your neighbors are those with whom you roam, though you will know very few of them personally.

- Promenade is an ancient and nourishing human activity.

- A united neighborhood can be a very powerful force.

- We each have a responsibility to take care of one another in our neighborhoods.

- Generosity is the foundation for a good life and a strong neighborhood.

- The commons belongs to everyone, and everyone is welcome to sit, promenade, visit, and roam. The commons is where it is easy to talk to almost everyone.

- Every person is precious and valuable and entitled to your fullest respect.

- The neighborhood is part of your personal village. Treat it well.

Resources You Can Use

Shabono by Florinda Donner, 1982

> Donner is an anthropologist who studied the Amazon Indian tribes. Her work led her to an old medicine woman, who said to follow her into the jungle. With no idea of where she was, Donner ended up living in an isolated stone-age village for almost a year. In the end she became one of the villagers. When she returned to civilization, she wrote about her experience of life in a hunter-collector village that could have existed 80,000 years ago. What she discovered will surprise, delight, and amuse you. You will enjoy this very readable book if you want to know what life was like for our ancestors.

Daily Life in Ancient Rome by Jerome Carcopino, 1969

> If you are a history buff, you will enjoy this very descriptive book about how the average Roman citizen lived, loved, and died in the company of his neighbors.

The Spirit of Community: The Reinvention of American Society by Amitai Etzioni, 1993

> Etzioni has written a definitive book calling for revitalizing community at every level of our lives. It is intellectual, comprehensive, and compelling. His work has started a revolution.

Extraordinary Popular Delusions and the Madness of Crowds by
Charles Mackay, 1841

> Not everything that happens in our neighborhoods is
> sensible. One hundred and fifty years ago Mackay wrote
> this very readable and fascinating account of the many
> ways in which crazy mob behavior sometimes becomes
> an epidemic leading to quite negative outcomes. If you
> want to know the inside story about the Crusades, the
> witch hunts in Europe, or Tulip-mania, just to name a
> few, this is the book for you. It will open your eyes to the
> potential dangers of being gullible and help you to live
> in your neighborhood with much more care. Currently
> in print, this book is still widely read.

***Home from Nowhere: Remaking Our Everyday World for the
21st Century*** by James Kunstler, 1996

> This in-your-face book will open your eyes to what mis-
> guided urban planners and developers have done to our
> personal lives by paving over America. Kunstler describes
> the mess we have made, and has mapped out how we
> can restore our urban environment. You will benefit from
> knowing what he has to say about how we design and
> treat our neighborhoods.

Chocolat, a film starring Juliette Binoche, 2000

> A delightfully playful film about a woman who sets up
> shop in the middle of a very conservative and in some
> ways calcified village, and by her simple loving and ac-
> cepting presence, plus a little magic, transforms the entire
> town for the better.

CHAPTER 6

Fellowships Open Doors

A fellowship is a gathering of people who share a common reason for being together, which offers a safe, low intimacy place to meet people. Finding the right fellowship for you requires that you first know the kind of people you want to be with and then search out places where those people are gathered. Once you find a fellowship, you can navigate from outsider to insider by taking your time, being persistent, and applying the strategies of showing up, hanging out, and taking part in the activities they offer. After you have appeared seven times you will become familiar. To connect yourself to as many people as possible, hang out with the most active and engaged people of the group and offer your skills to their joint efforts. Remember that it takes membership in several fellowships to maintain a diversified personal village.

Allison finally graduated from law school and took a job in a distant city where she did not know a soul. She was faced with the daunting task of reestablishing herself: finding a place to live, locating a good doctor, learning her way around town, and developing a platoon of friends who would support her. At first, the people in the firm were the only folks she knew. She started to roam, first in her neighborhood: the local grocery store and coffee shop. She scoured the newspaper looking for listings of events where she could get a feel for her new home. The Saturday Market, museums, art shows, and the old section of town became her haunts. Still, it was hard to form substantial connections easily.

She started to look for a synagogue. First she sampled the different synagogues in town. After a few tries she found one with an active young adult program. Applying the Principle of Seven she began to show up and show up again, and in time she knew quite a few people.

> *Fellowships provide a safe, low-intimacy place to start meeting people.*

Throughout our lives, we all will need either to rebuild from scratch or to revitalize our personal villages. It will happen when, like Allison, we move to a new place. It will also happen if there is a major change in our life, such as a divorce, a job loss, or a recovery from drugs, or simply from suffering through a midlife crisis or the adjustments of growing old. The journey of life takes us through many twists and turns that often leave us needing new people and new groups.

A fellowship provides a place where you can start at a low level of intimacy and gradually build relationships with the other participants, some of whom may become quite important to you. Once you become known, you will usually be able to find someone in the group who can help you get access to almost anything you will need. Do you need the name of a good dentist? Someone will know a good one. Do you need a good mechanic? Ask around in the fellowship.

Having a place where we belong and a place where we can become involved in something greater than ourselves nourishes our humanity. Most fellowships can provide these two. Involvement in the life of a fellowship can be food to nourish the fullness of life.

If you think of the neighborhood as a great park dotted with clusters of trees, rivers, lakes, open grasslands, and deep forests, you can think of the fellowship as an oasis rich in people and opportunity. The oasis is usually open to all who are interested. All you have to do is wander in and start showing up.

What Is A Fellowship?

A fellowship is a gathering of people who come together for a shared, common purpose. Usually fellowships have organized gatherings at a designated place with some kind of leadership, although it can vary from informal to quite formal. Fellowships provide a place to find a wealth of informal interaction. You will find them anyplace you find people. Different kinds of fellowships are churches, sororities, Alcoholics Anonymous (AA), the Rotary Club, the student body at a school, a well-functioning team at work, the Psychoanalytic Society, co-housing developments, wisdom councils, and Women in Black.

Women in Black is a loose fellowship that formed in 1988. Women in Israel began to don black and stand silently near the guard posts as a protest against the conflicts in the Holy Land. Soon others began to join them in their silent vigil. Like a breath of fresh air, the movement spread to Spain, Azerbaijan, Bosnia, England, and the United States. Now women dressed in black gather regularly in public places all over the world to stand silently in support of peace.

> *A fellowship is a gathering of people who share a common purpose for being together.*

Women in Black is a fellowship that grew spontaneously out of a need to restore harmony in our world. Any woman can join by simply showing up and standing the silent vigil in support of peace. If you want to find the Women in Black group in your area, simply search the Internet under that title and you will quickly find a gathering near you.

A fellowship serves as a hub. It provides an opportunity for people to meet and interact with others and then venture off in any direction with any person. Once you wiggle your way into the inner workings of the hub, all kinds of opportunities will be open to you.

Almost always, fellowships conduct some kind of formal gatherings in which you can participate, usually anonymously, as a way to scope them out. There is at least one fellowship for you, one that will meet your needs for a sense of community. But if you are like me, and probably Allison, the prospect of walking into a new place with a bunch of strangers is a bit unnerving. It is human nature to be uncomfortable with new people. The first time we encounter new people, most of us are on guard against being conned or laughed at or worse, ignored. There is a well-developed strategy to find just the right fellowship for you. It is possible to insert yourself into the inner workings, where you will be totally comfortable and feel at home. I will take you on a guided tour of the process. Of course if you are an extrovert you will already know all this, but for the rest of you—follow me.

How To Find The Right Fellowship For You

When you team up with good people, you become a part of something that will nourish you and everyone else at the same time. It is important to be careful whom you join with in this process. The company you keep will strongly influence your values and the kind of person you become. Let's look at how you can find good people to associate with in a fellowship.

First you need to know what you want for yourself. Of course that is not easy. Few of us have a totally clear idea about what we want in life. If you are not clear about what is important to you, then some homework is in order before you can go out and find people who share your passion. We don't have space in this book to fully explore how to do the self-inventory process to discover your life's passion and direction. But I can suggest a little contemplation that may help.

Knowing what you want is the place to start on your search for a fellowship that is just right for you.

There is a simple yet profound way to get some idea of where to focus your life.

Find a half hour of quiet time, and write down the following question: *What have I valued in my life up to this point?* Then, without thinking much about the question, write down whatever thoughts arise. Do this for a few minutes, and then close your eyes and ask your higher self to help you understand this question at a deeper level. Sit quietly for a few minutes, then write down what emerges from this contemplation.

Now write the next question: *If I knew I was going to die in five years, what would I want to do?* Again, brainstorm in the same way described above. After a few minutes stop writing, close your eyes, and again ask your higher self to help you understand the question in a deeper way. After sitting quietly for a few minutes, open your eyes and write down what emerged.

If you really want to go into this process, repeat the above procedure with these questions: *If I knew I was going to die in a year, what would I do?* and *If I knew I was going to die in a month, what would I do?* You can do this contemplation process with any question. It is a very effective way to tap in to your inner knowing and discover what is important to you.

Keep working with this general technique until you have a more clear idea of what you want and what has priority for you right now. Now ask the question: *Where would I find people who share my values and interests?* After you complete the contemplation process with this question, you will be well on your way to knowing where you are most likely to find people who share some of your common experiences and goals. When you can find people who walk the same common ground as you, a great magic begins to occur.

Once you know what kind of people you want to meet, you can locate fellowships by asking everyone in your network if they know where you might find the kind of fellowship that will satisfy your particular desires and needs. Other ways that you can find people who share your interest are a search of the phone book, newspapers, the Internet, or even asking shopkeepers for ideas. I once tested this idea out in a hobby shop.

At Forest Park Hobby Shop, I encountered Roy, a round-faced, potbellied man with soft eyes, the kind of guy you would expect to see in a Norman Rockwell poster depicting an old tire store in Vermont. I told him I was writing a book on how to meet people. I posed this hypothetical question: If I were interested in model trains, could he connect me with other people who were into trains? His eyes lit up. "Boy," he exclaimed, "Are you onto something. It's getting so there ain't no place to go to meet people unless you go to a bar and BS. And that ain't no good." Turning to a shelf behind the counter he pulled down a folder.

To find a fellowship, ask around in your network, go online, study the newspaper, or talk with a shopkeeper.

With growing excitement he went on, "I have all the listings for the model train clubs in the area. I can tell you exactly who to call, and you can have lots of friends. Seems a guy goes to work and someone tells him what to do all day. Then he comes home and builds these trains and creates his own world. And I can tell him who else is building trains, and they've both got friends. What kills people is these mail order places. Guys can order stuff at a good price, but they've got no way to meet others. Whenever I talk to somebody, I get his card or brochure. Then when somebody like you comes in, I can tell them exactly who to call. If a guy buys a model helicopter, I have a list of people who will teach him how to fly it. Then they all have friends." Roy went on like that for some time. With his help a person could be connected to a model train club—fellowship—in no time flat. So in your search for a group of people who share your passion, try the small shop keepers who are trading in your interests.

How To Sample An Existing Fellowship

Now that you have identified some good prospects, the next step is to evaluate what you have found. The best way to do that is to sample some gatherings. Here is how the extroverts and the networking professionals do it.

Keep in mind that most people are a little shy about meeting new people. As a new person, you are by definition an outsider, and insiders usually view strangers with caution. Your task is to become an insider. That means you will have to be patient and persistent, and keep showing up. This is what the professionals who connect with others for a living do. They show up, try as best they can to copy the manners and dress code of the group they want to join, and find a way to take part. They walk the walk, talk the talk, and learn the subculture of the group they are working to gain entrance into. Most people in an open fellowship like AA or the Chamber of Commerce will be welcoming. Yes, some people are too stressed or too busy or even cranky, and they may respond to your first approach with rudeness. Just remember they are in the minority. Expect to run into a couple of these, but don't get discouraged.

Navigating from outsider to insider will take time and persistence on your part. Keep showing up and take part in the activities of this fellowship until you decide if it is right for you.

Most fellowships are eager to have new members and will be quite welcoming. Often they have someone available to take you around, orient you to the activities, and show you where to hang your coat and what to do next. If possible, find that naturally friendly person in the group who will take you under his or her wing and orient you. That way you have the best chance of learning what this fellowship has to offer.

Bruce and Holly were committed to world peace, and before they moved to Denver they belonged to a very vital group of peace activists. In their new town they went looking for a similar group. It turned out there were several peace groups, which they located by calling local churches, searching the Internet, scanning the newspaper, and asking around. They went to several meetings just to get what I like to call a *felt-sense* of the people. But what worked best was when Holly called the coordinator of the Friends Service Committee to get the name of a person she could meet at their first visit. They went to a meeting and found her, and she told them about the values and politics of the group and gave them an idea of what the group could offer. By following this approach, they eventually found a group that seemed to match their values. Then they asked their contact person to introduce them to the key people in the group, who could help them find the most effective way to fit in.

Sometimes your initial contact in a new group is a special person designated to do welcoming, but more often, after you walk in the door someone will emerge from the group who will act informally to orient you to this new place. This person will be happy to introduce you to others. And more important, they'll show you where the bathrooms are located, describe how the formal meetings work, and tell you when they occur.

It is natural to feel like an outsider when you first start with a group. Be patient and don't give up too soon.

Keep in mind that during your initial sampling forays, you are looking for evidence that this group will be compatible with you and your interests. Since the people you first encounter will be representative of that community, your evaluation process can begin with them. The way these individuals interact with you will give you a hint about the quality of this particular group. If these people seem flaky or the group does not feel right for you in some other way, go cautiously.

Initially you will feel an uncomfortable, outsider discomfort. The best way to get past the initial feeling of being an outsider is to quickly find your way to the formal gatherings, services, classes, or demonstrations where you can sit quietly and observe. In time you will begin to see what is going on and know if you want to explore further with this fellowship.

Most groups are eager to have new members, and they may make a strong pitch for you to get involved right away. If they offer you an opportunity to take part in some of the activities, do it. This involvement will give you a better sense of whether they are your kind of people, and it will start to build up your seven-plus contacts in case you decide to continue with the group.

I must offer a word of caution. Some groups are organized around a strong issue that they feel passionately about. They want all the help they can get to carry forth their cause. Sometimes they are friendly simply because they want more worker bees, rather than because they are genuinely interested in you. This may meet your need perfectly, but on the other hand, if you want a sense of community more than you want to be another worker, then look carefully at what they have to offer. Other fellowships simply want converts, as many as they can get. When you walk into the door, they smell a hot prospect. If this is what you want, then you may have found something good. If not, keep your eyes open.

With some groups, it will be obvious that it is not the place for you. With others you may have to go back several times to get a feel for the energy of the place, the activities, and the people. Even though you will be using some objective questions to aid in your evaluation (these come later in the chapter), ultimately it will be your gut feeling about a particular gathering that will let you know if this is a worthwhile group in which to invest more energy.

Remember that even though these initial contacts will count toward the Principle of Seven, you are just getting started. At first you are there just to gather data, not to begin the effort to become an insider in earnest. Most people, including you, are vulnerable to feeling rejected and are sensitive to not being included. In the initial visit you may very well experience that uncomfortable outsider feeling and be tempted to judge the group based on that. Don't give in to this temptation. In order to feel like an insider, you will have to wiggle across the emotional boundaries of this particular gathering. Initially it is not the goal of the sampling to cross very far into the boundary of this group. It is to gather data. All newcomers are strangers and outsiders and, as such, feel uncomfortable.

SAMPLE SEVERAL GATHERINGS

Sometimes in a sampling foray you will find someone who warmly welcomes you, someone who leaves you feeling special and valued and included. That good feeling can be so wonderful that, rather than expend the emotional energy to explore another group, you may be tempted to leap right in and join the group. This is an error many people make when they do not believe themselves worthy of belonging anywhere. As soon as they find some place where they feel even a semblance of belonging, they stop right there and look no further. It may turn out to be a good choice or it may not. Enjoy the good feeling that comes from being included but do not let that stop you from carefully evaluating if this gathering is the right place for you. There are other criteria, besides simply feeling good or feeling included, upon which to base a decision to enter a particular group.

Sample many different fellowships before you begin to invest in one.

Do not stop at the first group. Even if you find a group that looks pretty good, it can still be a good idea to look over a few more. The additional sampling may confirm your decision that the first group was your best choice after all. When you find a fellowship that feels right, here is how you can be sure.

IS THIS GROUP RIGHT FOR YOU?

Now that you've found a potential fellowship, the next step is to evaluate whether the people are right for you, both in terms of what you want to be a part of and as folks you can relate to. Initially this will be a "felt sense." Once they pass this feeling test, keep exploring to see if this is a good group for you—because ultimately any group to which you belong will have to meet at least some of your needs. Attend one or more sessions of a group that seems promising, then take a few minutes and consider the particular fellowship in light of the checklist on page 113. You can use this checklist to evaluate any group you find yourself involved with, from family to work, to a coterie, to a fellowship. For now, we will use it as a starting place for the fellowship you are considering.

The questions on the checklist will serve only as a guide. Ultimately only you can properly evaluate if a particular circle is right for you. Listen to your intuition. Questions give your intellect something to work on while the real decision-maker, your intuition, comes to a conclusion.

During the sampling process, remember to be open to the possibility that this new fellowship is committed to something very vital that you had not yet considered. Be ready to expand your vistas when you enter a new arena. The delight and surprise of finding new things, people, interests, and opportunities will be yours if you can stay open.

By now you may feel that I am asking you to treat a potential fellowship with the same care that you would give to buying a car. I am. The kind of people that you team up with has a profound impact on your life. Choose carefully.

So You Decide To Try This Fellowship. What Next?

Start showing up. Attend the formal gatherings. Apply the Principle of Seven until it becomes one hundred. Learn the names of the people and remember them, even if you have to retire to the bathroom and jot them down in a notebook. The next time you meet, greet people by name. As they share about themselves, remember what they shared and refer back to it later. Having been remembered as a unique individual, this person will feel valued and will want to include you as an insider. Af-

If you want to become an insider, start showing up and build up your seven-plus appearances.

ter you do this with several people you will be an insider. Take part in their activities, volunteer to wash dishes or move tables or help with a mailing. Those informal shared moments help bond you into the inner workings of the group.

Almost every fellowship has small group activities, classes, committee meetings, or study groups. Join them and become an active participant. Yoko used this method to make herself included in a new fellowship.

She set out to find a spiritual fellowship and eventually found one that seemed promising. They offered classes, meditation, and yoga sessions based on an Eastern tradition that was interesting to her.

The group met on Wednesday evenings, so after work Yoko changed into something casual and headed to the meditation center. The first thing she did was to step into the flow of the evening program. The greeter at the door showed her where to hang her coat and where things were located. She found her way to the meeting hall, sat down, and waited to see what would happen next. At the conclusion of the formal program, the master of ceremonies gave a rousing welcome to all the newcomers and invited everyone into the community room for tea and sweets. Yoko followed this crowd of seemingly happy strangers. Several people came up to her and introduced themselves, though in each case they quickly exhausted their welcome-to-the-new-person repertoire and retreated to visiting with people they already knew. Soon Yoko was standing uncomfortably alone with only her teacup for company. She left.

The meditation program was exactly what she wanted, so she worked up her courage and returned. This time she found a table set out with books, so she stood there pretending to study the material while she sized up the feel of the crowd. Some of the same people came up to her again and made nice. Though she was slightly more comfortable than in the previous week, soon she was ready to leave.

On her fourth visit she noticed that the kitchen crew always called for volunteers to wash dishes after tea time. She decided to volunteer. In the kitchen, with water up to her elbows, the chatter was free and comfortable. She found it easy to enter into the banter and drift in and out of different conversations. She made it a point to volunteer to wash dishes every week after that. Soon she had more than just a "make nice" relationship with several people. Another time she volunteered to help with a mailing. As she sat at the table licking stamps and stapling, the conversation was easy and natural.

Now when Yoko went to a class or attended a yoga session, she felt like an insider. Not only did she have a spiritual path that made sense to her, but the people felt like hers. It took a while, but showing up, applying the Principle of Seven, and staying involved paid off.

HANG OUT WITH OBVIOUS LEADERS AND POPULAR PEOPLE

Any group you enter will contain a wide variety of people. Some will be outgoing and popular. Others will be the slightly shy, reliable standbys you can count on, and then there will always be a few loners and gossips. When you are an outsider first entering a new group, the fringe members, the complainers, and the troublemakers may spot you and try to draw you into their isolated or crazy system. At first you may not recognize them, but if you spot the leaders and popular people in the group and begin to hang out with them, you will not be drawn into any fringe element, if one does exist.

Every group has a few obvious leaders and folks who are easy to engage with. They are the popular ones who seem to be center stage or to be liked by a large percentage of the group. Sometimes they are the formal leaders, but more often they are the very outgoing and talented ones who rise to the more visible levels of the group. These are the people with whom to identify and develop a connection. Hang out with these people. They are the most effective at making introductions and weaving you into the inner life of the group. They are often the inner life of the group, so introductions from them to the other members and activities will be much more effective than if you let one of the loners or fringe people be your primary contact.

Multi-Strand

The weakest type of group is one where everyone is connected to the same central person but where the people do not have much connection to anyone else. Social psychologists call these single-stranded groups. These kinds of groups occur when a strong person dominates center stage, not allowing others to mingle and get to know each other. The group falls apart if that central person leaves or falters.

Conversely, the strongest group is multi-stranded, where everyone has a strong connection to everyone else. Do not let your involvement in a small subgroup cause you to stop interacting with others in the fellowship. Find any excuse to get involved with everyone. Learn all their names. Take part in activities with a large spectrum of people in this fellowship. Even if you are drawn into a small closed study or task group, do not limit your involvement to just those members. Reach out to as many people as possible so you are completely woven into the multi-stranded web of the fellowship.

> *A multi-stranded group is the strongest. Develop a relationship with as many people as possible.*

Residential Fellowships: Co-housing And Retirement Homes

Of course one method to envelope yourself within a fellowship is to buy your way into an already established community system. Josephine was recently widowed from her husband of 53 years. Her children and their families were busy. She knew she needed to create a community for herself. She solved it by moving into a home for retired teachers.

It took a while for the Principal of Seven to work for her. With time, Josephine gained recognition from the other residents. She still had to face the loneliness at night now that her husband was no longer with her. But she accomplished her task of entry into a tight, well-developed fellowship by buying into a home that was specifically set up to provide the type of community—among other things—that older folks need. The retirement community had a grief support group that met weekly, so she was quickly drawn into a loose type of coterie. Meals were served in the dining room twice daily, so she had an automatic daily ritual that placed her in contact with the other residents. One couple adopted her into their circle of friends. By the single act of moving into the physical territory of this specialized community, Jo set the stage for inclusion into a system where she could feel at home.

Frequently, when I tell someone I am working on a project to revitalize community, the topic of co-housing comes up. A growing architectural trend is to create living villages where residents have their own homes with small kitchens. Then, in small village style, they share a communal dining hall where they take some meals together, and they also share a large gathering room, laundry facilities, workshops, a craft center, and a library. A co-housing development is not a commune but a shared neighborhood fellowship that bonds the members financially and in many of the everyday activities of living. Co-housing is not for everyone, but if you are interested, set your search engine to *co-housing* and you will find an endless supply of links. The bookstore and library will also have many leads for you.

Fellowships Are Only One Of Your Important Places

A fellowship starts out on the low end of the intimacy scale. Some of your relationships might become very intimate with time, but most of them will be in that middle ground of affiliation. Remember to stay diversified.

Get to know as many people as you possibly can and take part in several different types of fellowships. Even if you have a strong fellowship, participate in more intimate groups like salons or coteries and maintain your connection to your family and close friends. One fellowship may open doors, but one fellowship does not make a personal village. There is much more. To deepen the level of intimacy with the people in your personal village, you will need lots of interaction and conversation. An excellent place to find good conversation is in a salon. A salon is more focused and potentially intimate than a fellowship. Lets turn our attention now to how those work.

Fellowship Evaluation Checklist

1. Do these people share in common with me the things that I value and find interesting?

2. Do I feel safe and comfortable with this gathering?

3. Do these people seem to be affirmative toward each other?

4. How do I feel about the people who are here? Do I like them? Do they seem to resonate with me in some positive way? Do they share a common intellectual bond with me? Do they share a common language and value system with me?

5. Do the physical surroundings, the dress code of the participants, and the language they use suit my taste and leave me feeling comfortable?

6. Do I feel that I could develop a sense of belonging within this gathering? Do the members treat each other as valued, special, unique people? How welcoming are they to me?

7. Does this group seem to contain some people whom others avoid or who seem to be troublemakers? (You will know this right away because you either will see it directly or your intuition will tell you that something is wrong. If you detect this, it could be a sign of trouble. If this situation exists, look closely before getting very involved.)

8. Do these people offer warmth and affection to one another without being inappropriate?

9. Is this group focused on larger issues that have meaning for me, or are they just focused on themselves and meeting their own needs?

10. How vital is this circle of people? Are they present to what they are doing, or is there an underlying depressed quality about this group? Did I come away from my time with them feeling revitalized, refreshed, and excited, or did I feel drained, down, and discouraged?

11. Do the members of this gathering take turns giving their best or do a few people dominate? (Pay close attention to this one. If a few people dominate, you may not have the opportunity to be competent in this gathering unless you migrate into a leadership role. In that case you may end up doing everything by yourself.)

12. Do these people seem to have a sense of integrity? Do I sense I could trust them? (The opposite here would be a group of people who are paranoid against the outer world or who are gathered together to take advantage of outsiders, or worse, to do them harm.)

IN SUMMARY

- A fellowship is a hub that opens the door to your people world.

- A fellowship provides a safe, low-intimacy place to start meeting people.

- A fellowship is a gathering of people who share a common purpose for being together.

- Knowing what you want is how to start on your search for a fellowship that is just right for you.

- To find a fellowship based on things that interest you, ask around in your network, go on-line, study the newspaper, and talk with shopkeepers.

- Sample many different fellowships before you begin to invest in one.

- Once you find the right fellowship for you, remember that navigating from outsider to insider will take time and persistence on your part. Apply the Principle of Seven and keep showing up. Take part in the activities of this fellowship until you decide if it is right for you.

- Use the Fellowship Evaluation Checklist on page 113 to evaluate any fellowship or group. Use it to make sure a particular group is working for you.

- It is natural to feel like an outsider when you first start with a group. Be patient and don't give up too soon.

- Keep showing up. In time people will start to interact with you and draw you into the inner workings of their gathering.

- Hang out with the popular people and the leaders.

- A multi-stranded group is the strongest. Develop a relationship with as many people as possible.

- A shared living situation like co-housing or a retirement home can become a powerful fellowship providing a foundation for your life.

- One fellowship does not make a personal village. Diversify.

Resources You Can Use

If you are puzzled about what you want in your life, let me suggest four books that will lead you through a process toward clarity and life direction.

How to Get Control of Your Life and Your Time by Alan Lakin, 1973

I Could Do Anything if I Only Knew What It Was by Barbara Sher, 1994

The Seven Habits of Highly Effective People by Steven Covey, 1989

The Purpose of Your Life by Carol Adrienne, 1998

How to Work a Room by Susan Roane, 1988

> The title of this book is misleading. It implies a manipulative approach when actually it is chock-full of tips on how to establish significant contact with strangers at a conference, a cocktail party, a church social, or a workshop. In short, it is a survival manual for how to navigate that tense situation of being in a room full of strangers.

Letitia Baldridge's Complete Guide to a Great Social Life by Letitia Baldridge, 1987

> This classic book is about how to meet people, engage in all kinds of conversation, make friends, and walk with grace through your social sphere. It belongs on every bookshelf.

Fidelity, Five Stories by Wendell Berry, 1992

This collection of short stories is a sample of one of America's clearest writers on community and the human experience. His stories about friendship, love, fellowship, neighborhoods, and the value of community are some of the best ever written. If you are not familiar with Berry's work, start with this book, and then go to the bookstore and browse over his rather extensive collection. You will find a treasure.

Boycott, a documentary film about the Montgomery, Alabama, bus boycott in 1955

In 1955 Rosa Parks refused to give up her seat in the whites only section of the bus. A cultural explosion erupted out of her stand, resulting in a boycott by the black population of the public bus service in Montgomery. A vital fellowship of black leaders emerged to support this stand, including an unknown preacher, Dr. Martin Luther King, Jr. You can watch the inner workings of a real fellowship in this film, which shows an event that changed American history and marked the beginning of King's career as a civil rights leader.

CHAPTER 7

Fine Conversation In The Stimulating Salon

Conversation is one of the threads that run through the fabric of community. A salon is a gathering of people who meet for the express purpose of having fine conversation. A leader or facilitator provides direction and the salon is often quite topic focused. You can start your own salon or be invited to attend one already underway. In the conversation, every person is given an opportunity to speak and be heard. Salons can be found in many places: in cafes, in living rooms, or around a campfire. A friend may invite you, or you can find them listed in the local newspaper, on bulletin boards, and on the Internet. In the salon your intellect will be stimulated. You will be introduced to new ideas and people, and you'll have great fun.

A salon is a center for lively conversation. Before we go into how they work and how to join or start one, we need to examine in detail the magic and dimensions of conversation. Since conversation is the thread that weaves us together in almost all human interactions, it is important to turn our attention to this topic.

The skill of conversation is more valuable than learning how to drive a car or work on a computer. You may have seen a young mother in the grocery store with a tiny infant strapped to her chest telling the baby what is on each shelf. No, that mother is not half a bubble off. She intuitively knows that the music of her voice is teaching her baby how to talk. The words the baby hears create neural pathways in its brain that later turn into language. Conversation begins very early.

> *The most satisfying conversation happens when there is a focus and the setting is a comfortable, familiar place.*

Lovers whisper in each other's ears. Neighbors gossip over the fence. Children chatter noisily. CEOs share how lonely it is at the top and trade fishing stories. When people knew they were going to die in the Twin Towers, they called home with the final words, "I love you." As we lie on our deathbeds, our loved ones express gratitude for our lives and wish us well on the journey. Conversation is with us throughout life.

In ancient Greece conversation was so valued that every home, from the most palatial to the most humble, had a special room devoted to conversation. They called it the *andron*. There the Greeks gathered for conversation, discussing everything from politics to the latest gossip.

In fashionable Parisian society between 1700 and the early 1900s, it was all the rage for people to gather for serious conversation in what they called *salons*. These gatherings were often sponsored by a well-to-do Parisian woman, who would set the time, place, topic, and guest list. Once the conversation began, she usually defined the rules of conduct as they discussed the topic of choice. Those who were impolite or disruptive were not invited back. It was partly out of this caldron of conversation that the French intellectual movement emerged.

In the modern world television replaces face-to-face conversation, and everyone sits in a special room where they listen to and watch others have conversations. Instead of engaging in conversation ourselves, we watch conversation. Of course we do join in conversations on talk radio, in chat rooms, and through e-mail, when we happen to have time in between our commutes, many meetings, and continual "busy-ness." The old parlor has fallen into disuse, and new architecture tends to replace the parlor—the *andron*—with TV and computer rooms. The conversation room is too often the couch, over which looms the television. When a conversation finally does get underway, a ringing telephone often interrupts. We are so accustomed to sound bites that our conversations tend to degenerate into drive-by comments as we zoom past each other on our way to the next event.

It is easy to imagine our hunter-collector ancestors sitting around the fire at the end of the day telling stories, repeating gossip, and joking. In fact, early anthropologists who studied the Bushmen in Southern Africa and the Aborigines in Australia reported that their evening conversations went on for hours and very closely resembled the intimate type of personal sharing and gentle prodding of a therapy group.

Our ancestors were experts at the art of conversation. Though this art may have become diluted, we can reshape it to fit into our modern life. The salon is one place where vital, stimulating conversation is nurtured and expected.

THE FOUR TYPES OF A FOCUSED CONVERSATION

Remember, the more you share about yourself with another, the deeper the intimacy between you. If you share with each other over a long period, there is a good chance you will develop a good friendship. Of course most conversation is small talk, gossip, jokes, or just catching up. This casual interaction is the lubrication that keeps social interaction flowing smoothly.

But if you want to have a stimulating conversation that takes you someplace, then you will use a combination of the four types of focused conversation. A workshop about conversation will often start by teaching the differences between these four major conversation modes: debating, discussing, solving/planning, and dialoguing. Conversation shifts back and forth between these four all the time.

Debating

Pick a topic—any topic—and choose one view. Another person takes the opposing side. Then the two of you try to convince each other that your position is the most logical one. These conversations can become quite lively and maybe even appear to turn into an argument. As long as they do not turn into personal attacks, these conversations can be quite stimulating and, for most people,

> *Debate: striving to get others to buy in to your position.*

fun. We all need debate skills when we are called upon to present our side of an issue. The skills necessary to present our position are very useful when we ask for a raise. The same skills used in debate come into play when we are trying to sell our ideas in a presentation to a city planner. Debating is

a high art and, when used as a tool to present your side of an issue, becomes a very useful skill to possess.

In our personal villages, however, we tend not to use debating very much. The debate process puts off many people because it feels too much like a hard sell. If debating is sport for you, but you sense your conversation partner is pulling back, then you had better shift to a different process. If you persist it may seem to the other person as though you were at war, and he or she will not want to become a casualty.

Discussing

The root meaning of discuss is to *take apart, to shake up, to dissolve.* So when you need to examine something, discussion is the process of breaking it down into its parts and examining each one to come to some new understanding. Sorting through the pros and cons of an issue or a problem is the process of discussion. When you go to the marriage counselor, probably you will spend quite a bit of time discussing (examining) your communication styles and the underlying intentions behind what you and your partner are saying.

Discussing: dissecting an issue and examining every aspect.

Francine and Russ bought an old house with the intention of completely transforming it into their dream home. They asked an architect, Mark, to help them think through what they wanted. Mark led them into a discussion about their lives, their dreams, how they had inhabited their homes in the past, the importance of physical, acoustic, and olfactory privacy, and how much and what kind of private space they each needed. This discussion led into a solving and planning type of conversation. In the end the house design included many little rooms that would give them privacy, but when the doors were opened, created a large commons for entertaining.

Solving And Planning Conversations

We all have solving and planning types of conversations at work, when organizing a wedding, or when dividing up the chores. You know the process. First identify the items in the task, then prioritize them and decide who will do what. This process can range from planning a menu to preparing a climb up Mount Everest. If it is about a problem, like how to get someone into alcohol treatment, then the discussion about the best way to convince a person to do something he doesn't want to do can be very lively and intense. Together you will weigh each possibility and examine the best way to help, even though the person will be resis-

Solving and planning: using discussion and developing an action plan to solve a problem or accomplish a task.

tant. After that, you will come up with a plan and agree on who is going to do which part. Usually you will not find much of this kind of conversation in a salon, though some salons do evolve into taking action about something the group has all discovered as a shared passion.

Dialoguing

Dialoguing is a type of conversation that is not goal oriented. The intention of dialogue is simply to bring harmony between people, while leaving room for differences. It is usually stimulating, exciting, and very satisfying.

With dialogue, everyone is working to hear clearly and without judgment what the other is saying. Each person speaks without challenge. Each individual's statement is valued and added to fuel the fire of the conversation. The goal of dialogue is common understanding.

> *Dialogue: listening to others without judgment, to discover the common wisdom of everyone present.*

As the participants in a dialogue grow to understand each other, an electric process of discovery, intimacy, and movement into new realms of meaning unfolds. The rules for dialogue are simple. Listen fully and without judgment to what each person says, and then add what you have to say while the others listen fully to your truth at that moment. Everything said is okay. All statements are left on the table to be considered and responded to by others.

Dialogue might move into problem solving and even include some discussion, though usually it does not involve debate unless everyone agrees that is what they want to do. Often dialogue is the listening and inquiry process that comes before a task-focused conversation. There is no room for control or domination or mean-spiritedness in dialogue. If you try these, you might be kicked out of the room. Dialogue is the type of conversation usually found in salons.

WHAT IS A SALON?

The origin of the word salon comes from the Latin *sala*, meaning a hall. In Old Italian it grew to refer to a large elegant room where receptions were held or where distinguished people gathered. In France the word was transformed into *salon,* meaning a gathering of people who talked about topics that were important to them. In frontier America the word morphed into *saloon,* which referred to a place to drink spirits and have conversation. More recently *salon* has come to refer to a place where you have your hair done. Hair will still be done in salons and producers will still make movies of people drinking in saloons. But the way we are using salon here is more like the way it was used in Paris two hundred years ago. It is a social form that has slid into the background of modern times. Now it is being rediscovered as a vital place where people can find stimulating conversation.

Elaine once brought to her women's group a collection of quilts that had been hand sewn by several generations of women. Some of the quilts first came into being by candlelight. Later, others were sewn together under kerosene lanterns. As the women sat in a circle, Elaine spread her quilts out one at a time. Sitting in a circle, the women held each quilt and talked about those who had made them. As they talked, it was almost as if the energy of those earlier women came into the room. The emotion stored in those quilts brought tears to everyone's eyes.

Were these quilting bees salons? Well, sort of. At least the quilts gave the women a focus as they talked about their lives. Shared effort had created the quilts that the earlier women needed for their families, and they gave these women a reason to be together as they talked. I would tend to call these circles sharing centers. But if the women agreed to explore a specific topic, then I would call it a salon. The distinction is somewhat blurry.

In the 1970s, women gathered to discuss how to enhance their position in society. Now here was salon—vital conversation—which eventually brought power to women and change to our culture. That same period brought encounter groups, where people attempted to be as real with each other as they could. Sometimes these conversations were focused on a specific topic, so we would call them salons. But most of the time encounter groups were psychological immersions, sometimes emotional free-for-alls, where everyone was encouraged to disgorge their feelings, often without any consideration for others. It was a period where the operating procedure was *get it all out*. Encounter groups are not what we are talking about when we speak of salons. Encounter groups still exist, but mostly they have evolved into something hosted by a facilitator or a therapist.

We call it a salon when a group of people gathers at a specific place with a host who holds the focus and protocols for conversation. The goal is to come together to dialogue around a specific topic. Salons generally happen repeatedly over time. Remember the Principle of Seven. Repeated contacts build something vital.

THE STIMULATING SALON

Third Sunday

Ann reached up into the hat and pulled out a question. Unfolding it, she read: "Have you ever been to a psychic? Do you think they are real?"

Ed replied immediately, "Oh sure, I see a psychic. She seems to know things that blow me away. It's good. I think she is for real." And with that the group was off, with each person sharing his or her experience of psychics and what they thought of them.

Finally Sherrie said, "That was my question. I made an appointment with a psychic and I have never been to one. I wondered if I was crazy or something." To which everyone chimed in that she should go and listen with her intuition to what the psychic had to say. And then they pulled another question out of the hat.

Jose and Joanna host this particular salon. Meeting the first Sunday of every month, their procedure is quite simple. They open by inviting everyone to write a question to put into the hat, and before they begin Jose reviews the rules about how to hold a salon conversation. You will find those rules on page 133. The hat is passed around, one at a time the questions are pulled out, and the dialogue begins. Unless the writer of the question claims ownership, the group does not ask whose question they are discussing. Each person must respond briefly so that everyone has a chance to share. All questions are respected and all responses are respected as being the truth of that person. Asking questions about or challenging what someone said is minimal. Instead, each person responds to the question on the floor with what springs from inside. If the conversation drifts away from the intent of dialoguing about the topic on the floor, Jose or Joanna will bring it back into focus. Jose keeps the time so each question gets its fair share of attention.

Here is a sample of typical questions.

- *What qualities make civility more likely, and is civility always a virtue?*
- *Do you pray? Why? What's your definition of prayer?*
- *What do you hope for and fear regarding our new president?*
- *What is your favorite joke?*
- *Are you in favor of capital punishment?*
- *How do you deal with the increasing feeling of powerlessness we all experience in the world?*
- *What would you like people to say about you at your funeral?*

Jose's and Joanna's salon is open to anyone who is willing to stick to the rules. They put out an open invitation by word of mouth and their e-mail network. A steady core of the same folks comes every time, with a few new people each time and irregulars dropping in occasionally.

They solve the problem of latecomers by starting with an informal gathering over a potluck breakfast that lasts for half an hour.

By the end of that time, most of the participants have arrived and written their questions. Then they begin with little interruption.

The Gathering

Many years ago I invited a select group of dancers, artists, philosophers, psychologists, and group facilitators to meet, with the express purpose that each person would take a turn to do their thing with the group. One week we danced with Fanshon. The next week we did a guided fantasy journey into our inner realms with David. The following week John laid out his paradigm for society on the blackboard. And so it went—week after week. After each presentation we allowed time to dialogue about what came up for us. For the most part the same people came every week. People came when they could but participation was not mandatory. In all, about twenty people participated in the salon over a two-year period.

The Secret Society

Garrett, a high school teacher, invited all his fellow male teachers to a secret society meeting at his house one evening. There he proposed they spend the evening sharing stories about their lives and the concerns they had about the world in which they lived. At that first meeting the conversation became so lively that they agreed to do it every month. The men made a big joke out of it by advertising broadly that the secret society was meeting, when and where, and that only men were allowed to come and no one was to know that it was happening. This group continued to meet like this for several years, with lively conversation between the men who showed up each evening. Garrett took the role of holding the focus so the conversation would not degenerate into small talk, political debates, or arguments.

Mystic Beach

Just across the street from the antique Sylvia Hotel on English Bay in Vancouver, British Columbia, is a public beach, traversed by a classic promenade that goes on for miles circling Stanley Park. The entire setting looks like something out of a Gay Nineties lithograph. One day while on vacation, my wife and I wandered out of the hotel and ventured onto the promenade. In time we came to a groomed section of beach where a man was raking the sand and someone had obviously pulled the driftwood into a circle. Where the promenade circled this little refuge, I noticed a woman watering flowers. She had carried in earth and planted a small flower garden in the sand next to the promenade wall. I recognized that something organized was happening here, so I stopped to introduce myself. The woman with the flowers told me her name was Lelani and that she was a ballet teacher. She spent her summers helping her friend Jamil tend this section of beach. They informally called it Mystic Beach. Jamil was shy about my obviously journalistic interest in his activity, so Lelani told me his story.

Jamil lived in one of the high-rises facing the bay. Every day he'd come down to groom his adopted section of beach. It was like his front yard. And during the summer season he and Lelani would host a sunset gathering every Thursday, and I was invited.

It was then that I noticed they had put up a sign along the side of the promenade inviting everyone to come to an evening of conversation. It was Thursday, so that evening we showed up. Lelani and Jamil set up a beach umbrella, erected a light-tree out of a piece of driftwood upon which they had arrayed candles, and lit a fire in the middle of the conversation circle. Each week Jamil picked a topic for discussion. This week it was *Is peace possible?* For the next three hours, as the sun went down and the sky turned from orange to yellow to gray to star-filled, inky black, we sat with strangers we would never see again. While shadowy figures paraded by on the promenade just behind us and the surf gently lapped over the rocks nearby, we quickly became engaged in a most interesting conversation about peace in the world. Occasionally someone would emerge out of the dark to join us in the circle of candlelight. It was luscious. It was magical.

Jamil and Lelani had created what they called a *cafe conversation*.

Cafe Conversations

Cafe conversations are a form of salon. Usually a cafe will schedule a time when tables are set up, each with a different topic hosted by a facilitator. People can simply drop by and drift from table to table as they are drawn to a particular topic of dialogue. Salons in restaurants or cafes work the same way that the Mystic Beach conversation worked. Many cities and towns have cafes that offer this type of salon. Often a non-profit group devoted to good conversation will stimulate cafe conversations by enlisting restaurants to set aside a special time and a few tables. The sponsoring group will post a listing of the restaurant, the time, and the topic in the newspaper, on the Internet, and on bulletin boards. You can find these on the Internet by searching under the topic *cafe conversation* or *table conversation.*

E-Salons

Does your schedule, location, or discomfort about sitting in a room full of people interfere with your desire to join a salon? Never fear. E-salons are the thing for you. You can find them easily by searching the Internet under the topics *salon, discussion group, cafe conversation,* or *table conversation.* You will find almost any kind of discussion group you could ever want. E-salons lack the stimulation of close face-to-face conversation, but they do allow those people to participate who are more comfortable with this format or who are unable to find or form a local salon.

Book Discussions

A book discussion group is a close cousin to a salon. What makes book discussions different is that they usually are closed to drop-in members and participants have to do some homework to prepare. The specific book they are reading usually defines the topic for discussion. Sometimes though, the conversation ranges out to larger subjects and the book group turns into a salon type of experience. In general, book clubs do not have quite the electric and exciting quality of the more spontaneous salon; however, both are valuable. If you want to get started with the salon idea but don't know where to begin, a good starting place is to draw together several friends with the agenda of discussing a book. Or if you don't want to start one yourself, put a bug in the ear of a friend who is a natural organizer to pull one together, and invite yourself to come. Ask everyone in your personal village if they know of a book club that is open, or scan the newspapers for possible groups. On the Internet, a search under the topic *book club* or *book discussion group* may turn up something in your region that will be just right for you.

THE SALON IS SPICE FOR YOUR LIFE

For many people, a salon is the most stimulating forum they will have with other people. This is because when a diverse group gathers together, they bring with them a broad spectrum of experience and wisdom.

Why would you want to attend a salon? Not only will it stimulate your intellect but it will also introduce you to new ideas and new ways of thinking about old problems. As you meet new people and build up your seven-plus contacts, these relationships will strengthen and grow. The salon is an excellent place for expanding your personal village. It's also fun.

In a busy life where conversation tends to be brief and hurried, such a gathering is usually experienced as a refuge for a hungry soul. Salons are available to almost anyone who wants to find one. On the other hand, a few people find their way into an entirely different kind of forum where conversation can become quite intimate. That is the coterie I have been mentioning as we have gone along.

What is a coterie? you may ask. I'll devote a whole chapter to that later, but for now we'll define it as a small, closed group of people who meet regularly and whose purpose is to give each other support. It is a very private little group that continues to meet for years. A salon is usually more open with more members, and attendance is usually optional. Eventually you will want to find your way into a coterie to give your life depth.

Though the salon will never become the center point of your personal village, it will certainly add a degree of stimulation that you might not find anywhere else.

Now let's turn our attention to the question that everyone has: How do I turn the new people I meet into friends?

Conversation Guidelines

Share your own experience. Tell your own story. Avoid telling someone else's story. Speak your truth. Respect what every person shares as his or her truth. Let that truth stand on the floor, and add your own truth. Be careful not to criticize or attack what another has said or shared. Instead, add what it stimulated inside of you. Let the collective wisdom build.

This is a conversation, not a lecture. Keep your comments brief so everyone has a chance to share. Be careful not to turn your response into a sermon. If you want to give a lecture, save that for another place. Simply speak about what springs up inside you in response to the evolving conversation.

Every response is the right response for that moment.

Sometimes people will share things about themselves that are quite private. Hold what they share in confidence.

If a deep feeling arises inside you, own it. If you get overwhelmed with emotion, you can share it or take a time-out. You do not have to rescue others from their emotions. Usually it is best to sit with feelings rather than try to do anything about them. This is not a therapy group.

Remember that conflict is simply an expression of differences. Each person has a truth that might be different from someone else's truth, and strong feelings can arise. Let the differences stand and keep searching for the deeper truth that is trying to emerge in the conversation.

Never forget that each individual in the circle is a unique person with hopes, dreams, disappointments, and strong feeling for themselves and others. They are in this conversation because they want more vitality and connection to themselves and others. Be gentle and welcoming and kind to everyone.

Be careful that you do not take the dialogue off on some tangent without the consent of the group. If you are in doubt, ask others if they want to go in that direction.

Speak as you are moved. You can pass anytime you want. Listening can be a very powerful experience and a contribution to the circle.

IN SUMMARY

- Conversation is a thread that runs all through the fabric of community.

- The most satisfying conversations always happen in a comfortable, familiar place.

- Focused conversations take four different forms.
    1. Debating: striving to get others to buy into your position.
    2. Discussing: dissecting an issue and examining every aspect.
    3. Solving and planning: building on discussion to develop an action plan, to solve a problem or accomplish a task.
    4. Dialoguing: sharing and listening without judgment to discover the collective wisdom around a topic.

- A salon is a gathering convened by a leader at a specific place with the purpose of having a dialogue about a particular subject. You can easily start your own.

- A salon usually meets regularly and has both a focus and someone to keep the conversation focused.

- Salons are usually open by invitation, often to anyone who wants to come. They are found in many places and are relatively easy to locate.

- A cafe conversation is a salon in a public place at a specific time with a leader and a specific focus. It is usually a one-time event. You can drop in and table-hop.

- Salons can stimulate your intellect and introduce you to new ideas and new people, and they are great fun.

RESOURCES YOU CAN USE

Salons: The Joy of Conversation by Jaida N'ha Sandra, Jon Spade, and the Editors of *Utne Reader*, 2001

> The editorial staff at *Utne Reader* has taken up the torch of reintroducing salons into our culture. If you intend to start a salon, buy this comprehensive handbook about salons, their history, how they work, and how to make them work for you. It will become your bible.

Conversationally Speaking by Alan Garner, 1980

> You will find many books on conversation, but Garner says it all in this very readable and clear book. A sample of his table of contents includes Asking Questions that Promote Conversation, Listening So Others Will Talk, Starting Conversations, and Letting Others Know Who You Are. This is a great book if you want to improve you skill in the art of conversation.

Dialogue: Rediscover the Transforming Power of Conversation by Linda Ellinor and Glenna Gerard, 1998

> If you are a professional group discussion leader in search of a comprehensive handbook with much practical and technical information about conversation and dialogue, this is an excellent source for you.

Internet sources

> The Internet. Set your search engine to *salon, salon conversation, table conversation, cafe conversation, commons cafe,* or *conversation circles.* This will open an endless supply of links you can use.

Utne Reader magazine

Many issues are devoted to the topic of community, salon, conversation, and issues relevant to living in today's world. It is packed full of useful information that you can use to make your life work better. If you are not familiar with this resource, pick up a copy at your newsstand. You may want to subscribe.

Dead Poets Society, a film starring Robin Williams, 1989

A fellowship of boys in a private high school forms a salon. It started out as a lark, but in the end they are all transformed. If you want to see a real salon at work, watch this classic.

CHAPTER 8

From Stranger To Casual Friend

Meeting people and developing relationships from scratch is an art you are learning as you read this book. In the beginning, common ground is your license to engage. That initial common ground will gradually expand to include other common interests and places as comfort develops between you. Initially you are best advised to keep your focus on learning about this new person and not overwhelm him or her with too much self-disclosure. With a new person you may freeze up and be unable to think of what to talk about. A few memorized icebreakers will solve that problem. Stay in public places until you know you can trust this new person to treat you with respect. And be available when this new person reaches out to you, if you want something to develop further. Let the relationship become what it will become as it develops. You both may be pleasantly surprised.

By now you have a feeling for how to roam in your neighborhood and in fellowships, and maybe you have even found a salon for some stimulating conversation. Perhaps you have noticed that in all these places, you found strangers wall-to-wall. For some people, it is easy simply to turn these strangers into familiar strangers and then into acquaintances and, in some cases, into friends. But if you are like lots of folks, it is not so easy. There is an art to making the transit across the intimacy continuum that is natural to some and well known to the networking experts, but for a lot of us is a complete mystery. Vern certainly was puzzled by that art.

He and John were walking along the beach on the Oregon coast when they noticed a particularly curious geological formation. It teased the junior scientist in them to explain its origin. At the base of this formation was a man intently chipping away with his rock hammer, apparently equally puzzled.

As they drew closer, John asked the man if he knew how this rock had formed. Vern watched as the two of them entered into a fascinating conversation about geology. Eventually John asked the man if he lived nearby. That question led the rock chipper to describe how his grandfather had built a cabin here long ago and it had evolved into the family retreat. He had been coming here since he was a kid. John asked, "Are you a geologist?"

"No, I'm just an amateur," was the reply. "This rock has puzzled me all my life. Maybe I'll figure it out someday."

At that point John reached out his hand and said, "My name is John, what's yours?" That led to a round of introductions. Then John asked what the man did in the outer world when he was not chipping rocks.

"I'm a school administrator in Portland," he said. John explained that he too was a college administrator, so they traded notes for a few minutes before John wished him well with his rock. As they walked away, Vern turned to John and commented that he wished he could just walk up to a stranger and start a conversation like that. John shrugged and smiled as if to say there was nothing to it.

It's likely that John was not consciously aware he was using a shared common curiosity with the stranger—how this rock had formed—to open the conversation. He made it more formal with a name exchange, then broadened it out to find out how the stranger happened to be here—he lived nearby—and finally what he did outside of this context. There you have it, the simple formula for starting from scratch with a stranger and nudging the relationship toward something more substantial.

The Three-Step Formula for Starting from Scratch with a Stranger

1. *Start with what is obviously common to both of you.*
2. *Develop a first-name relationship.*
3. *Gently troll for information about other shared common ground into which the two of you could expand.*

Beverly was equally puzzled by Rhonda's ability to do this. They were both family therapists, and in their weekly breakfast at Julia's restaurant they gradually had grown to recognize the regulars who also ate there. One woman in particular had caught their eye. One day Rhonda recognized a book this woman was reading, so she walked over and began a conversation. After a few minutes Rhonda returned to Beverly and announced that this person was also a family therapist and that she was reading one of the new books in the field. This new acquaintance and Rhonda had decided to meet for lunch the next day to talk further about their therapy practices.

Just like Vern, Beverly envied her friend's ability to walk up to a stranger and start a conversation, particularly one that led to a follow-up meeting. Rhonda was unable to tell her how she did it, except to say that she just started talking. Beverly wanted to know if she could learn this ability. The answer is yes.

How To Develop An Acquaintance

Both Rhonda and John were applying basic strategies that any-one can learn. When John began to talk to the rock chipper, for instance, he applied the principle of starting with a common ground. That is, he initially engaged around their shared common curiosity about the rock. Then John explored for other common ground by asking if the man lived nearby. After that he applied the strategy of developing a first-name relationship, and then broadened out in a gentle way with curiosity about the man's life beyond the beach.

Rhonda, on the other hand, simply applied the strategy of inquiring about a common interest—the book—and expanded their conversation from that. Her contact was brief and set the stage for another brief contact. Without knowing it, both John and Rhonda were using the techniques we've been discussing. Keeping the initial contact brief, they started with common ground, learned and used names, and expressed curiosity about the new person. You never know what you will discover. John and Rhonda had the good fortune to discover a much larger common ground between themselves and the new person: their work.

Even more fundamentally, they were using the basic mindset of being purposeful and persistent. Rather than waiting for the other person to come to them, they each reached out. It is doubtful whether the rock chipper would have reached out to John and Vern on the beach, but after John's purposeful initiation he was eager to talk. And the family therapist in the restaurant may have been interested in Rhonda and Beverly, but she may not have been able to think of a way to engage them. The book and the fact that they were familiar strangers in the same restaurant provided enough common ground for Rhonda to reach out to her legitimately.

THE COMMON GROUND IS YOUR LICENSE TO ENGAGE

Common ground is the reason people are together in the same place. It gives people license to talk with each other. In Rhonda's case, one major shared element that gave her permission to approach the woman in the restaurant was that they were familiar strangers. By this I mean they had spent so much time in the same place that they shared face recognition. Having the same taste in restaurants and frequently eating breakfast at the same time was another common factor. The fact that the woman was reading a book that only a family therapist would read was the clue that a significant common ground was shared.

The conversation probably went something like this. Rhonda said, "Excuse me, but I've been hearing about that book and wonder if it's any good." After an obvious positive response, Rhonda went on to say, "I'm a family therapist, and I assume you are too if you're reading this. My name is Rhonda. What's yours?"

By introducing herself, asking for a name, and learning a little bit about the work they obviously shared, Rhonda expanded her knowledge about their common ground and invited more engagement. We can imagine Rhonda going on, "My friend and I come here frequently for breakfast and we've noticed you. Is your office nearby?" Again Rhonda was staying with the obvious common ground. She built upon her newly found information that they shared the same profession. Then she could have easily said, "I'm always interested in expanding my network. Would you be interested in meeting for lunch so we could talk more about our work?" Her initial brief contact made an opening for a follow-up meeting.

The common ground is your license to interact.

This technique of starting with the common ground is the universal and natural way to engage. For example, when strangers are thrown together in the workplace the common ground of the job is clearly defined and engagement is automatic and easy. By being purposeful and persistent, you too can engage with a stranger if you keep your initial contact focused around obvious and immediate shared issues. This approach is the starting foundation upon which you can expand the comfort between you—by building up familiarity. As you use a series of brief interactions, you also build up to your initial seven contacts.

MOVE FROM THE OUTSIDE TO THE MIDDLE

Remember the intimacy continuum? The more you share of yourself, the deeper the intimacy can become. Initially you are on the stranger end of the intimacy continuum. Then you become a familiar stranger and finally an acquaintance, as each of you finds out more and more about the other.

By sharing a series of brief interactions with a new acquaintance, the two of you develop an anchor in a shared place around some shared interest or activity. Take your time. If you rush a new relationship, you may rush them right out the door. Pace how much you disclose about yourself in the initial phases of the relationship. Peggy had an experience where she got overwhelmed by too much self-disclosure from a woman.

What Peggy noticed most about Ellie when she introduced herself at the neighborhood picnic, was that her arms, legs, and torso moved as much as her lips when she talked. In no time, Ellie was telling Peggy her troubles with her alcoholic husband and the difficulties in her marriage. Then she began to talk about her alcoholic father and how, as a sexual abuse survivor, she was having to learn how to set boundaries. Finally when Peggy was able to break off the conversation gracefully, Ellie expressed an interest in talking more in the future. As she walked away, Peggy rolled her eyes as if to say, "No way."

> *Always start at the edge of a relationship and move gradually toward the center.*

One difference between an acquaintance and a friend is the degree of self-disclosure. Initially, as acquaintances, we run the risk of scaring people off by telling too much about ourselves. As we move toward being friends we will share more about our personal lives. Always start at the edge of a relationship and move gradually toward the center. That means start with the common ground and engage around issues that are important to both of you, only gradually sharing more intimate details about your life as they are relevant.

As the example of Ellie demonstrates, when you are first introduced it is wise to share only superficial things like your name, a little of your personal history, and what brought you to the same place. Share personal but non-intimate things, like your age, family status, the general area where you live, how long you have lived there, and what kind of work you do. Let this new person know only what is relevant to the business of your being together. If you share intimate material about yourself too soon, your new acquaintance may feel pressure to do likewise. As we saw earlier, many people are fearful that their underlying sense of inadequacy will be exposed if they reveal much about themselves. By proceeding slowly, you protect yourself and them from this fear.

Until you have developed some connection beyond the immediate situation that brought you together, it is best to let the other person set the pace about how much is safe to share personally. If he or she seems uncomfortable at your level of sharing, you can back off until more trust has developed.

Now you may encounter another problem. We live in a world of self-centeredness. We have all been around people who are so full of themselves they never seem to notice that we even exist. Jennifer met a fellow student during her studies in political science. This student attached herself to Jennifer and then revealed an annoying habit of engaging Jennifer by immediately starting to talk about herself. Every time they met, this woman would talk excitedly about her studies in international relations and how she was going to change the world, or some other wonderful thing about herself. Jennifer grew to dread this woman's approach because she felt she totally disappeared by Ms. Talk-About-Myself. This is a worst-case scenario with a self-centered person.

When meeting new people, however, you may run into this problem in a different way. If you tell too much about yourself too soon, you may convey to this new person that you are a narcissist who is only interested in them as an audience to their greatness. To protect yourself from giving this wrong impression, maintain an attitude of curiosity about the new person and pace your self-disclosure. Of course most of the new people you meet will also inquire about you and your life. But do not expect this kind of give and take initially. Keep your focus on the other person. When they return the favor, you will be delighted.

Be Endlessly Curious

Curiosity about your new acquaintance is the approach that will open many doors. It is one of your major tools for developing contact. Most people like to talk about themselves and they feel valued when someone shows an interest in them. Faced with the degree of self-centeredness that exists today, you probably have noticed how difficult it is to find anyone who will truly listen to your story. The new people you meet are no different. They will feel valued when you are genuinely interested in them. Of course you will need to reciprocate with some things about your life, otherwise you will appear to be a reporter going after a story. As you share with each other, the growing common base will make it much easier to deepen your mutual contact.

Many people will be as nervous at the first meeting as you are, and it may not occur to them to be interested in you because they are self-conscious. They may be so relieved to have someone show an interest in them that they will begin to talk about themselves and get carried away. If that happens, it does not necessarily mean that you have a narcissistic personality on your hands, so do not immediately become discouraged.

If you freeze up with a new person, come prepared with a few icebreakers.

Unfortunately, many of us blank out when meeting new people. Our spontaneous natural curiosity disappears in the face of our nervousness. This happens because at a deep level, we fear that we will be discovered as inadequate or we fear the risk of embarrassment in saying the wrong thing. This very common experience leads to that familiar new-person freeze-up.

There is a good way to deal with this blanking out. Come prepared. Memorize a list of questions you can use to learn about a new person. After the initial contact is established, a degree of comfort will develop and then your natural curiosity will return. Here are some of the questions I use until my spontaneity takes over.

Some Freeze-Up-Protection Questions to Remember as You Meet a New Person
- *What brings you to this place?*
- *How long have you been coming here?*
- *How do you know (our host)?*
- *Where do you live?*
- *Have you always lived there?*
- *When did you move here, and where did you come from?*
- *Where did you go to school?*
- *What kind of work do you do?*
- *How did you get started in that line of work?*
- *Do you think you will do that work the rest of your life?*
- *What do you do for fun?*
- *Do you know a good doctor, dentist, mechanic, cafe?*
- *Where have you traveled to recently?*

If you go to one of those dreaded cocktail parties or receptions where you do not know a soul and would like to hide in the closet, this approach of inquisitiveness may save you. When you can draw out even a part of a person's history, you will be surprised at the fascinating stories you'll hear. It's delightful how interesting people can be. You may not meet a single person with whom you would want to spend more time, but you will leave with an expanded understanding of other people and their lives. That alone will add roots to your personal village. Your life will be enriched.

I remember how my friend Renee came into my life. I first noticed her at the morning break of a Psychoanalytic Lecture Series one Saturday morning. An obvious newcomer to this group, she was standing quietly near the cookies, coffee cup in hand, watching the crowd. Our eyes met and she said, "Hello," and introduced herself. She told me this was her first time here and wondered if I had been coming for a while. Soon she had me talking about the Psychoanalytic Society and its history, and the next thing I knew she was listening with great interest as I told her about my work. She shared a little bit about herself, but nothing intimate. At one point she asked if I would introduce her to some of the other people.

The next month she remembered my name and inquired about my work. I was delighted to be considered important enough to have these details about myself remembered. We shared a little more about our work and moved on to other people.

As these brief contacts accumulated at subsequent meetings we grew increasingly comfortable with one another, and before long I thought of her as a regular. After several months she suggested that several of us go out for lunch following the morning lecture.

Renee was applying several of the principles for developing acquaintances out of relative strangers. She started from the shared common ground of psychoanalysis, was persistent, remembered names, kept showing up on our turf, and showed an endless curiosity about us. In time her persistence and patience resulted in her being known as a regular in our fellowship. Renee skillfully moved herself from stranger to acquaintance, and was well on her way to having several casual friends in the process.

MOVE FROM THE COMMON GROUND

After you have developed some rapport with a new person, you may want to expand to new common ground.

Doug and Jeanette did just that. Their first contact came when they were assigned to the same assembly group for an electronics firm. For many months they worked side by side at the test bench, bantering, cracking jokes, and learning about each other. After some time Jeanette was ready to expand this relationship by asking Doug to join her with some friends.

If she had invited Doug to a party the first day he went to work, he might have accepted but perhaps with some discomfort about her aggressiveness. He might have wondered, What gives with this woman who invites unknown men to parties, and does she do this indiscriminately with all men? As a result, suspicion could have been an initial part of their relationship. Instead they built a base of trust and comfort on the initial common ground, the job site, so that expanding to new activities and territory was the next logical and easy step.

Engaging in the established rituals and activities of the place where you first meet helps to build a sense of security. By staying in the familiar territory for a while and using the established group's language and customs, you create an atmosphere of comfort that allows the other person to learn about you easily. Once you know each other you will want to expand to new ground, which includes new territory, activities, and rituals.

> *Expanding to a new common ground takes the relationship to a deeper level.*

Peter and Dean met as fellow firefighters. As they grew acquainted through their shared work in the fire station, they discovered that they were both amateur carpenters. Peter spent a day off helping Dean build a new bathroom. Then Dean spent some time helping Peter dig out his basement. Moving from the shared fireman experience to a new arena, home improvement, provided additional ground upon which they could build a deeper friendship. From that new ground, with clearly defined activities—painting, digging, and sawing—they began to expand the base of their relationship naturally. Now the intangible something that marks the difference between a casual friend and a true friend could begin to grow, rooted in the fertile ground of their shared passion for carpentry.

EXPAND TO A PUBLIC PLACE

Spending time in a private place with another person implies a certain degree of intimacy, sometimes more than we are ready for early in a relationship. A good way to make the transition to a wider common ground is to expand your activities into new but still public territory. Most people first meet in public and will initially limit their activities to other public places, like a cafe, the theater, a group activity, or a conference. The rituals and structure of the public place will continue to provide a protective envelope of familiarity and security.

Public places are lower on the intimacy scale. As you move into more private space, the potential for intimacy grows.

Nicole, a bank executive and a reserved woman with a strong sense of dignity and decorum, had just moved to Atlanta. One of her first tasks was to begin a search for a new personal and professional network. At a management conference she met Janet, who seemed like a potential friend. They traded war stories about women in industry and agreed to meet for lunch. Their relationship expanded to further lunches, and eventually Nicole invited Janet to her home for dinner, a more intimate affair but still public with their husbands present. As their acquaintance evolved toward friendship, they began to spend more time alone going for walks, attending the theater, and sharing confidences. Until their friendship was well established, all of their contacts had been in public places.

A friendship is a private affair. Moving too quickly to private activities and territory implies a degree of intimacy that may not yet be appropriate. By choosing a public setting as you expand your common ground, you protect the two of you from any unnecessary discomfort that can occur in an intimate private space. If your comfort level or your intuition tells you to go slow, then stay public. Many people who do not listen to this inner voice get into trouble.

A WORD OF WARNING

Many times we connect with people who are very interesting and engaging. However, it may not be wise to move to the intimacy implied by being in a private place with them right away. The reason may simply be a personal issue of comfort and pacing, or it may involve the potential of being robbed or even hurt. Unfortunately, a few people who initially appear to be quite trustworthy later turn out to be dangerous. We all need to be careful, yet we cannot live in a fortress either. Women, children, older people, and yes, even men, need to be very careful not to go into private spaces with a new person until they are very sure they will be safe and will be treated with respect.

People who run into trouble were often hurried too quickly from a public place to a private place, before they had enough information to know whether they would be safe. For whatever reason, they were rushed and did not have enough time to assure themselves that their integrity would be respected. Had they been able to stay longer in the place where they first met and then expanded their time together into public places with other people present, they might have noticed behaviors that would have told them that violation was possible. Though this is not a crime prevention handbook, there are certain warning behaviors to watch out for when you are first getting to know a new person. See Potentially Dangerous Behavior Checklist on page 158.

If any of the items on the warning list rings a bell with someone you do not know well, then stay public. We warn our children not to get into cars with strangers. Police recommend that older folks do not let people into their homes until they are well known. Rape prevention manuals describe one seduction process where a man is super friendly and warm, engendering immediate trust. Very soon he invites his victim to a private place—a car or an apartment—where there is no escape from crime.

By staying public you protect yourself from potential harm by ill-meaning people until you can take their true measure.

Annette tells about a time when she was a teenager riding the bus to school.

She became very friendly with the bus driver, who one day offered to pick her up at school and take her to lunch. Annette's friend had recently taken a class in rape prevention and, watching this interaction, became alarmed. She described to Annette the typical seduction process and asked her not to meet him. Annette could not believe this nice man could mean her any harm and dismissed her friend's warning. Annette's friend went on to explain that if the driver offered to take her to his home, trouble was brewing. Her friend persisted, so Annette agreed to meet the driver at a local cafe so she would not have to get into his car, and she insisted on paying for her own lunch so she would not be obligated in any way. In the crowded cafe the driver did indeed extend just such an invitation, and Annette politely paid for her lunch and left. Who knows what might have happened had she not been careful.

We all need to be careful. Do not go to someone's private quarters, take someone to yours, or get into a car alone with someone unless you know the person will treat you with respect. With personal safety such an issue in our culture, you will be very wise to take extra time and stay away from private places with new people until you are quite sure you will be treated with goodwill.

Fortunately, this dire warning only applies to a small minority of the people you will meet. Most people are to be trusted, and your careful use of pacing will prove and develop mutual trust. Keeping commitments is one of the major ways of doing just that.

Nourishing A New Relationship

Keep Commitments

The development and nourishment of trust is an important dimension in any relationship, either new or established. Trust is built on many factors, and commitment is a major one. Shelly recently met a former colleague at a conference. Over lunch they reestablished contact and he agreed to call soon to set up another meeting. He never called. His failure to keep his agreement did not go unnoticed. Though Shelly was somewhat interested in spending more time with him, she was consciously testing his degree of commitment to their relationship. When he did not initiate contact, she realized he was not invested. Shelly did not reach back.

We are constantly making contracts with each other. For example, Todd asks Sandy, "Would you look up Willie's phone number for me when you get home and call me right back?" When Sandy calls, she fulfills the agreement she made. A tiny grain of sand is added to the mountain of trust. If Sandy forgets because she is preoccupied, however, a tiny grain of sand may be removed from that mountain. Todd may say nothing or he may ask again, but he notices. He may feel not valued, or he may feel hurt or even

> *Trust is the bedrock on which relationships are built. Keeping commitments builds trust.*

sabotaged. Of course we all forget sometimes, but if we are chronic about violating our agreements, either large or small, we erode trust.

In developing a relationship, we build trust if we commit to only those agreements we know we can keep and then make a serious effort to follow through. If you tell Cathy you will meet her for breakfast, you had better be there if you want her to be waiting for you the next time. If you and Joe are developing a relationship over fishing and he makes an agreement to pick you up at 5 AM, it is important that he be on time. Based on your agreement, you crawled out of your warm bed early. If he drags in at 6:30 saying, "I'm sorry, but I slept in," you know right away that sleep is more important than his commitment to you. If Joe does this repeatedly, your relationship may derail.

If you make an agreement that you cannot fulfill, call and rene-gotiate. Your budding friend will feel valued by your consideration. If something happens or you truly forget, get in touch as soon as possible. Explain the situation and either do what is necessary to keep the agreement or ask what you can do to make it right. Again, you convey your intent to do well by your agreements. Trust will flourish with such an approach.

Be Available When Your New Acquaintance Reaches Out To You

Mike grew up in a dysfunctional family where he learned that intimacy often resulted in betrayal and pain. He did have the ability to hang out with people, however, and was quite a likable chap. One woman was drawn to him, so it was natural for her to invite him to a gathering of friends. The possibility of intimacy implied by her invitation made him very nervous. He made up the excuse that he already had an engagement and retreated. This happened over and over until she finally stopped calling him.

Mike obviously needs therapy to resolve his intimacy avoidance issues, but his mistake illustrates a pattern to be avoided. You have put a lot of work into making yourself available and visible so that others can be comfortable with you. When they reciprocate, go out of your way to be available. When they begin initiating, it is a clear signal that you have passed the first milepost. If you want this rela-tionship to develop, be available when this happens.

Of course you cannot always be available. If you cannot accept the invitation, respond in some way that indicates the relationship is important to you, like, "Oh I'd love to, but I can't make it at that time. Could I take a rain-check, or could we find another time to do that?" When the tone of your response to their reach-ing out is "Oh yes, I'd love to," the other person will feel affirmed in their effort. Often that reaching out was accomplished with some anxiety on their part. Your positive response leaves them feeling welcomed and keeps the door open. If you want a closer friend, you had better be available when this new person reaches out to you.

Be Inclusive

As we saw earlier, self-centeredness is a major problem for many people. When an individual is too wrapped up in himself or herself, other people seem not to exist. Of course all of us are self-centered in some ways, but a certain use of language is a sure tip-off that self-involvement is excessive.

The overly self-consumed person will too often use the personal pronouns *I* and *me*, and seldom use *you* or *us* or *we*. Use of self-centered pronouns tends to work against closeness, while the inclusive pronouns *us* and *we* help to build a sense of inclusion. Language has a signaling function, and this narcissistic use of language does not signal interdependence and mutual involvement. Simply using the pronouns *we* and *you* and *us* will encourage warmer feelings between you and others, and will make others more likely to want to spend time with you.

If your budding new friend calls to invite you to attend a beach party after finals and you respond with, "Oh I can't, I have to meet my mother at the airport," you convey that your mother is very important, but the response does not acknowledge the status of your relationship. A *we* response would go something like this: "Oh dear, we've got a problem. I want to go to the beach with you, but I have to pick up my mother at the airport." This conveys that your new friend is important also, affirming the mutual quality of your relationship. Inclusive use of language is one of the ways to affirm your budding friendship.

LET THE RELATIONSHIP BECOME WHAT IT BECOMES

This chapter has been devoted to describing the initial steps of building a friendship. Yet most of the people in our personal villages will never become more than familiar strangers, acquaintances, or casual friends. Nurture these relationships because they are also important to you and to the other person.

If you are searching for a certain type of relationship, it may be difficult to allow a new budding friendship to be something different from what you had in mind.

The successful author Jane Adams uses the image of boxes. She points out that some people have a box which they want to fill with a certain kind of person, often a mate. They search here and there, desperately trying to find someone to fill that particular box and rejecting as unsuitable anyone who does not fit their criteria. In fact they may meet many perfectly wonderful people who could be assets in their lives, but since these people do not fit into the box they are trying to fill, they quickly move on and do not develop potential friendships. She points out that our more significant relationships usually emerge out of our pool of acquaintances and casual friends.

> *We need a wide variety of relationships. Let each one find a place within your personal village in its own natural way.*

If you are experiencing some frustration or disappointment with a new person, it may be a signal that you are pushing for something that is not right. You may be trying to fill one of your boxes, into which this new person does not fit.

If the type of relationship you had hoped for does not evolve, admit your disappointment and try again with someone else. Remember that most relationships fall somewhere between acquaintance and casual friend. Accept what did evolve as a valuable addition to your personal village. You two may always be good acquaintances and have much to offer each other. That is a gain. You need the breadth of ideas and opportunities that acquaintances and casual friends can bring. After all, you do not have the time to nurture more than a few deep relationships. If you have succeeded in developing a new acquaintance, you are better off. A good friendship may develop later.

On the other hand, if you have the good fortune to have a relationship that is going deeper, I have some things to share with you in the next chapter that will be useful to the two of you. These are ideas that would help a marriage or a friendship or even a business partnership. In fact this next chapter on developing depth in a friendship would be a good one to share with your mate, friend, or colleague.

Potentially Dangerous Behavior Checklist

1. Do you feel somehow uncomfortable and can't put your finger on why? Your intuition is trying to tell you something. Listen, be cautious, and stay public.

2. Is this new person impulsive, lacking the patience to let things develop? Is this person in a hurry?

3. Is this new individual pushing you to make a decision or to take action?

4. Does he or she fail to keep commitments?

5. Does this new person exhibit nervous, agitated, or strange behavior? Inappropriate laughter or loud talking is a tip-off.

6. Any individual who is using drugs, including alcohol, or appears to be using them may be a risk to you.

7. View with caution any individual who is very friendly and seems to act as though the relationship was more intimate than your time together warrants.

8. Is there anything in this person's past behavior that is questionable, regardless of what explanations are offered?

9. This bears repeating. Do you feel somehow uncomfortable and can't put your finger on why? Your intuition is trying to tell you something. Listen, be cautious, and stay public.

In Summary

- Meeting people and developing relationships is an art form that can be learned.

- The three-step formula for starting from scratch with a stranger is:
    1. Start with what is obviously common to both of you.
    2. Develop a first-name relationship.
    3. Gently troll for information about other shared common ground into which the two of you could expand.

- Initially engage a new person around the shared common ground. That common ground is your license to engage.

- Start at the outside, superficial level of the relationship. As the relationship develops, you can move toward more self-disclosure.

- Pace your self-disclosure to protect yourself from premature exposure and to give the new person time to size you up.

- Focus the conversation initially on the new person, until he or she begins to reciprocate.

- Be endlessly curious about this new person.

- Come to a new encounter with a few ice-breakers in case you freeze up.

- Move to new common ground to deepen the relationship.

- Be cautious with new relationships. Some people are dangerous and can cause harm if you are not careful.

- Initially expand to a public place.

- Stay in public until you know you can trust this new person.

- Keep your commitments as a way to build trust and goodwill.

- Be available when your new acquaintance reaches out to you.

- Be affirmative by using us and we pronouns.

- Let the relationship become what it becomes.

Resources You Can Use

How to Start a Conversation and Make Friends by Don Gabor, 2001

> A very practical, plain language book that will take you by the hand and teach you step-by-step how to engage with new people. It is a gold mine of in-the-trenches tips for starting a conversation with a new person and leading that relationship toward something valuable for both of you.

Brief Encounters: How to Make the Most of Relationships that May Not Last Forever by Emily Coleman and Betty Edwards, 1979

> This comprehensive book contains a practical chapter about "How to Talk with Practically Anybody, Anywhere, Anytime," along with a wealth of practical steps for developing a relationship that may be brief or may last a lifetime. It is full of the wisdom about relationships that has stood for thousands of years.

Power Networking: 55 Secrets for Personal and Professional Success by Donna Fisher and Sandy Vilas, 1991

> Salespeople, bankers, businessmen, and all professionals who work with people have to know the skills that allow them to meet people and develop relationships. This skill is the life-blood of their work. Written in plain language, this very clear book takes you to the very center of those skills. When you know how the professionals develop relationships, you will be equally as successful in your personal life.

I and Thou by Martin Buber, 1970

> This is the classic philosophical text written in the 1930s about two people in relationship. It is an intellectual jewel that has been treasured for generations.

Starlight Hotel, an Australian film starring Kate Robson and Patrick Phelps, 1987

> A touching, tender story about a teenager who ran away to find her father and a man fleeing the law for a crime he did not commit. The simple common ground of two people on the run draws them together. The resulting relationship that evolves as they meet many adventures on their journey across the length of New Zealand will stick with you. It holds many deep lessons on the process of creating a relationship from scratch.

CHAPTER 9

Roots In Friendship

A true friendship has a special, almost magical quality about it, and is limited to those few people who are high on the intimacy scale with you. It takes commitment and hard work by both parties over time to turn a relationship into a true friendship. Good friends challenge each other to be their best and stand by to support each other's unfolding life stories. People who have two or three confidants are happier and more productive in life. Friendships are intensely private and at the same time a community asset. Your close friends are the treasures of your personal village.

Whom would you call if some terrible thing happened in your life and you needed the help and support of someone you trusted? Stop right now and make a mental note of who comes to mind.

On the flip side, whom are you so committed to that you would drop everything and immediately fly to her side if that friend were in sudden need? You know the situation. These are the people we turn to when a close friend or family member is suddenly very sick or in a serious accident. This is what the social psychologists call your sympathy circle. For most of us, this list is very select. Usually between five and fifteen people make this list.

Of course your close family members would be included, but there are also a few cherished friends who are so committed to you that their names come right to the top of the list. If you have not done it already, take a few minutes and write down the names of the people in your sympathy circle.

Your Sympathy Circle

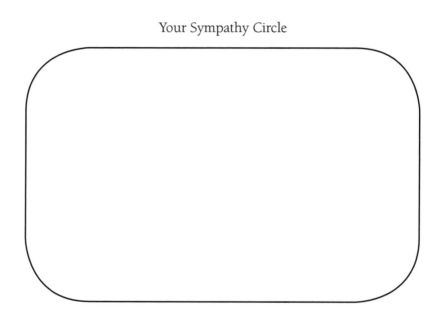

Most people can count on the fingers of their hands the number of very deep friends they have had in a lifetime. At any given time, we have only a few friends like this because they take so much time to maintain. If you could not think of anyone to write down on your list, then apply the lessons of this book and in time you will have a close circle of people to call on in any situation.

Of course you have many friends who range down the intimacy scale, and often some of these will appear in your sympathy circle for a period. In time most of the friends who cycle through your life will drop away—some in a few months, some after a few years—and a very small circle of friends who will remain with you for a lifetime. A rooted friend is very high on the intimacy scale because over the years you two have shared so much: rituals, activities, aging, total familiarity with each other's physical space and emotional experiences. Your deep knowledge of each other has grown and grown until you grok each other.

Do you remember we talked in Chapter 3 about what it means to grok? To grok another person is to know his or her inner experience as if it were our own. To grok yourself is to know your true self so well that you totally accept yourself as you truly are, both the wonderful things and the limitations. It is not necessary to share intimacies or emotional storms in order to grok. Grokking comes naturally when you hang out with someone over a long period of time. Gradually the two of you come to know all of each other's annoying characteristics and magnificent greatness. And as a result each of you accepts both dimensions as if they were your own. That is true friendship.

A true friendship does not happen with everyone. You might find it in your marriage or with a workmate or colleague or neighbor or with your daughter. You know it is there because your hearts soar whenever you are together.

The Purpose of Friendship
- *To give our heart a place to rest.*
- *To support the unfolding story of our life.*
- *To challenge us to grow and become our best.*
- *To give us a place to play.*

Once in a while on your journey through life, you turn your head and realize that a spark has ignited that magical something between you and another person. Perhaps that spark ignited very early in your relationship. Or sometimes it took a long time before you realized a powerful magic was at work between you. This magic is different from the familiarly and comfort that comes with sharing a common ground and rituals. A true friendship is absolutely enchanting. As a line from a classic song goes, "Make new friends and keep the old. One is silver and the other gold."

The nature of your friendship will depend upon the context the two of you share. If you are married, then you have a context where the potential exists to become best friends for your entire life. If you have a context where you become confidants, that may also offer you a friend for life. Sometimes a friendship will spring out of the most surprising situation.

True friendship has a magical quality about it.

Charlene was a potter who made her living as a massage therapist. Paulette wrote mystery novels. She found her way to Charlene's massage table after an auto accident. Charlene was single and Paulette was married with three children. Their lives were so different that, outside of the massage room, their paths and interests never crossed.

But on the massage table they began to grok each other through physical contact, and in time they began to talk about the two things that they did have in common: their shared spiritual quest and their mutual enjoyment of frank conversation. Paulette valued Charlene's healing touch so much that even after her body healed from the accident she kept coming back for more massages. In time they began to talk about their shared quest to know God and other topics near to their hearts. Their mutual delight at being in the company of another person who would tell it like it was drew them together into a bond based solely on Paulette laying on the table and Charlene working on her body while they talked.

Eventually Charlene invited Paulette to look at the work in her pottery studio. That broadened the context a little. Both of these women grew to feel delight in each other's presence. Sometimes Paulette would take a break from the massages for months on end, but something always drew her back to Charlene's table, where the bantering and sharing took up as if they had seen each other the previous day.

Their friendship existed for over twenty years only in the narrow context of their massage table conversation. Then one day Paulette called for a massage, to hear a message on the voice mail that Charlene was ill and unavailable. Paulette did not think much about it until a year later when the phone rang and a feeble voice came over the line. "Paulette, this is Charlene. I have something to give you. Could you come by?"

Paulette knew something was wrong, and she mentioned that she had heard the message from a year earlier saying Charlene was ill. Paulette wanted to know the story. Charlene responded by telling her that she had developed bone cancer in her leg and could no longer work. She wanted Paulette to drop by so that they could talk, and so she could give her something.

Charlene met her at the door, hunched over a walker, looking very thin. She wanted to give Paulette one of her sculptures and she wanted to talk. The frank conversations that the two of them had enjoyed over the years were what she needed just then. She told Paulette that the doctors did not give her long to live. She was hoping that Paulette would be willing to drop by occasionally while she went through this part of her life.

Suddenly the context changed for these two women who had grown to be very close grokking buddies over the massage table. From then until Charlene passed away, Paulette was often by her side. Of course Charlene's own rich community surrounded her during this time. But the ability to speak frankly about the ultimate goal of the spiritual quest and about death was a unique and sacred bond between these two women. We never know when a true friendship will evolve out of an unexpected context, or how that context may change until we live it out.

It is good idea to assume that every relationship you are in has the potential

Treat every relationship you are in as if it has the potential to turn into a life-long, bonded friendship.

to turn into a life-long, bonded friendship. You will not be drawn to every person you meet, but given the magic and the opportunity and enough time, the potential for intimacy may be there. You cannot know which relationship will spark, so you will be wise to treat all of your relationships with great respect and care. You never know which one will become one of the treasures of your personal village.

A FRIENDSHIP IS A SACRED PLACE TO REST YOUR HEART

When I say a friendship is sacred, I am not talking about religion. To me, sacred means precious, to be held with great respect and reverence. Abdi grew up in Iran, before he moved to America. In Iran he learned the value of reverence and respect and dignity in all his relationships.

One day he called his friend and in his typical Persian way he said, "Hello William, this is Abdi. I called to hear the music of your voice. I tried a couple of times last week but you were not at home, and I did not leave a message. I was driving home from the bookstore and I thought, it is Sunday evening and maybe they are busy, but like a pot with a dry plant that needs water I decided to call on the chance that I could hear your voice. Your voice is like the rain to me. It is so nice to talk with you."

"Abdi. It is I who is watered. The pictures I took of you the last time you were over are sitting on my desk, and I feel blessed by gazing on your wondrous form every time I sit here," replied William.

"Oh I am so sorry that you are put to such misery to have to look at such a dreadful sight," countered Abdi.

"Quite the contrary. I am blessed being reminded of you as my friend and remembering how much I love you."

So in a way that is not typical of American men, Abdi and William affirmed their relationship.

These two friends constantly affirm their love for each other and recognize the depth of what they have. After a little chat they agreed that the pot was now watered and that they would soon find time to get together. They find refuge in each other's company. Their friendship is a place for each of them to rest their hearts.

What does it mean to have a place for your heart to rest? We have two hearts. One beats in our chest with unfailing regularity. The other is the name we give to that tender, vulnerable place within all of us where we hold ourselves and others dear. That heart is the source of our love, our compassion, our creativity, and our spontaneity. The heart is the divine center from which our life springs.

When we are centered in that divine heart, we know our true beauty and strength and creativity. We know that we are truly loving and perfect.

This part of ourselves is so precious that we will protect it from assault with the ferocity of a Kung Fu master. One common way we protect our divine heart is to cover it up with a false self: a script that we act from and which, in time, we grow to believe is our true nature. The whole topic of scripts by which people live their lives is way beyond this book, though it is well described in the self-help literature. I'll name a just few of the more common scripts.

- *The Lone Ranger: I'll do everything myself without your help, thank you (so I won't have to feel the possibility that you might fail me).*

- *Tyrant: I'll scare you away (before you can hurt me).*

- *Truly Sweet: I'll charm you with sweetness (so you will like me and not recognize that I really see myself as ugly and unworthy).*

- *Helpful: I'll always be available to help you at any cost to myself (so maybe you will feel like helping me someday).*

In time we grow to identify with our script and come to believe that it is who we truly are. We have forgotten that our true nature is loving, compassionate, strong, creative, spontaneous, and generous. When we identify with our script rather than with our true nature, we are always at work protecting ourselves from hurt or disappointment and there is no rest. When we allow ourselves to trust another person, then we let down our guard and become who we truly are. We open our heart. When our heart is open, we can see our own beauty because we see the reflection of the beauty this trusted friend sees in us, and we draw closer to each other. This is what I mean when I say a friendship is a place to rest your heart.

A trusted friendship allows you to be who you truly are without having to defend yourself by retreating into some false self-script. In a true friendship, it is possible to allow yourself to be truly beautiful, happy, sad, angry, annoying, or forgiving. It is a place where you can let down your defenses and share your self-doubts, hopes, pains, disappointments, failures, and inadequacies, while knowing that you will be accepted for whatever you bring to the relationship.

> *A friendship is a place where you can let down your defenses and share your self-doubts, hopes, pains, disappointments, failures, and inadequacies, while knowing that you will be accepted.*

Usually it takes a long time to develop enough equality on the initial common ground for two people to become true friends, but not always. It is possible for people who have known each other for only a short time to be true friends, but it is unusual. The longer people have known each other, the more likely it is that they have learned to set aside their scripts in each other's presence. Without the scripts, mutual respect and a true heart connection are possible. If a quick connection happens, it is often when two people share an intense emotional experience. The intensity of the experience they have shared creates a positive intimate anchor between them. They can have something quite significant if they build on that initial anchor.

Dave and Rebecca met and were soon struck with Cupid's arrow. They were madly in love, and that initial passionate obsession created a strong anchor between them. They got married with all the naive dreams that they would live happily ever after. But, as usual, it was not so easy. They had to plow through all the stages in the relationship, from honeymoon to disappointment and struggle—even fighting occasionally. Eventually they grew to grok each other and filled their lives with friends, play, rituals, and meaningful work. They both came to accept that the other had annoying aspects which they would never like, but they could eventually come to live with and accept those qualities. Out of this fertile ground they learned how to be their true selves in each other's presence. Though it has not always been easy, they have grown to be each other's best friend.

Everything I have been emphasizing in this book, including hanging out together over time, observing the virtues, and being persistent, are tools that you will use to develop friendships. Even though I have been talking about applying all these principles and strategies to developing a well-balanced personal village, they apply particularly well to laying the groundwork for truly deep friendships. When you apply everything we have covered in this book to your marriage, to your relationship with your children, to your colleagues, and to your close loved ones, then you and your loved ones will enjoy a great bounty.

> *It takes time to develop a true friendship—a lot of time.*

FRIENDS SUPPORT EACH OTHER'S UNFOLDING LIFE STORY

Our life story is continually being written. With the support of our friends, that life story unfolds toward greater integrity and greater wisdom. We would not easily trust ourselves to venture into vulnerable places of growth without the psychological and physical holding and security that a friend can give us.

Dennis and Gil are two social psychologists who have created an astounding friendship that is rare in both its depth and its caring. They have cried in one another's arms as each went through a divorce, and they've hiked, fished, sailed, danced, and worked together as psychologists. They have stood by each other as death and tragedy visited their individual lives, and they have challenged each other to be honest with themselves and with each other.

Dennis and Gil met during a professional training program, as Dennis was making a career shift from professional dancing to psychology. He was feeling that typical outsider discomfort when he walked into the classroom for the first time. As he put it, "I didn't know anyone and was feeling pretty nervous and alone. I was checking out the other people there because I knew I had to connect with somebody. I remember being drawn to Gil. He was sitting on the couch with his arms sprawled out on both sides like he was welcoming me."

As the year progressed Dennis and Gil had many opportunities to learn about each other. The training program was designed to teach about emotional processing by having the participants explore their emotions with each other as part of the experience. One day as Gil was sharing with the group his grief over the recent death of his daughter, Dennis quietly walked behind him and began to massage his shoulders. Together they cried over Gil's loss. That sharing of grief began a profound bond between them.

The training program combined three years of study and personal discovery. All of the students grew close, but a special affinity developed between these two men. They fondly remember the informal times together with their fellow students where everyone laughed and danced and hammed it up. The program became an intense community based on exploring relationship issues, self-expression, and deep emotional sharing. It was in that context of openness and community that their friendship sprang into life. When the program ended they continued to meet weekly to hike, sail, and share intimately about their lives. Eventually they became business partners.

A TRUE FRIEND CHALLENGES US TO BE OUR BEST

Dennis and Gil know about resting in each other's hearts and supporting each other. They also know about the necessity of challenging each other. They challenge each other to get real. Gil remembers Dennis confronting him as he tried to smile his way through the pain of his divorce. "My God," said Dennis, "I wish you would not be so damn cheerful when you are in all this pain. You're obviously hurting. Would you just go ahead and cry?"

Gil remembers that moment. "It was wonderful. Dennis' words were all it took for me to feel my loss and let down." After that, they agreed that they would be real with each other as long as they both felt good about it or could stand it or bear the pain.

Ricco puts it a little differently. She uses the metaphor of layers to describe her close friendships. A successful financial planner and a woman surrounded with a strong circle of friends, she explains it like this: "There is a purity of soul or inner self in each of us. Everything else is a layer, like the onion. These layers act like prisms that distort our ability to see out clearly from our pure self to others and to the world. When we are in a close relationship that is committed to honesty and being real, then we have a chance to discover our distortions and we can begin to relate from the pure self."

A true friend challenges us to be real with ourselves and with them.

Ricco continues. "I assume that my friends are coming from that pure self, so when they challenge me I listen because I know it's an opportunity for me to learn where I am being defensive, and as a result I know I am not being honest with myself. The way I know that my friend has hit upon something important for me is when I feel something. Usually it is pain, like embarrassment or fear, but that just tells me my friend is close to the truth about me. It is the pain I share with my friends that opens our hearts to each other."

Apparently it works, because her friendships have depth and great closeness. When we are stuck in one of our scripts, then a good friend is the one who points it out and nudges us. From a place of wanting the best for us, they urge us to look at that part of us that we would rather not face. When we discover who we are with another person, we open up to ourselves and to the other person. When a close friend can be trusted to hold in private what we share, we call them a confidant.

CONFIDANTS

Social research shows that people who have a confidant outside of their primary relationship enjoy better mental health. On the surface that sounds good enough, but the question may arise: *Do I have to betray my parent or wife or partner in order to enjoy the benefits of having a confidant?* Not at all.

Remember Charlene the massage therapist? She and Paulette shared many confidences over the years. Once while Paulette was questioning her marriage, she talked with Charlene about her struggle. Charlene listened and drew Paulette out a little but she did not express her opinion or take sides between Paulette and her husband. Instead she did what a good confidant does. She listened and held what she heard without judgment, without taking any action or giving any advice. This allowed Paulette to hear her thoughts aloud as she processed her own struggle. Ultimately she was able to think about the problem in a way that allowed her to talk about it directly with her husband.

Confidants listen without judgment and without taking any action or giving advice.

That is what confidants do. They act as a sounding board without taking any side and without judgment. It is not easy to hold back your own response or to suppress your advice at these moments, but a mature confidant is able to do this. When a field of trust has been established between two people, so that what they each say will be held in confidence and without judgment, a rare and precious friendship has evolved.

HOLDING YOUR FRIEND

Psychologists talk about holding another person's emotion. Sometimes we have an emotional experience that overwhelms us. It is hard to know where to place that feeling inside. When we try to hold—all by ourselves—something that is emotionally difficult, we may compensate by becoming sick or developing anxiety or depression. When we share that hard thing with another, then two people are doing the holding (sharing the feeling) and we are better able to bear the weight of that difficult experience. When a counselor helps a person debrief from a trauma, this is a good part of what is going on. A good confidant does the same thing. He or she holds a psychic space for us that is larger than ourselves, where we can explore and process painful things.

We need to treat all of our friendships with confidentiality if we want trust to grow. If you take it upon yourself to tell everyone what you heard or to take sides and gang up on someone, then you are not a confidant, you are a meddling gossip. In time you may wonder why your friendships falter. A friendship is a sacred field within which the two of you hold each other with great respect.

> *We need to treat our friends' confidences with respect if we want trust to grow.*

It is worth your while to devote some energy to nurturing two or three of these friendships in your life. When you keep what every friend says in confidence and hold it with reverence, then you are acting with integrity. Some people will respond in kind and then you are moving toward becoming mutual confidants. You cannot say everything to just one person. By letting several people hold the precious moments of your internal state, you spread out the holding and no one person experiences all the stresses.

Sometimes you may need to talk through an issue that is beyond what your friends can bear or handle, or you may not want to burden your friends. Then you turn to a counselor or therapist.

This professional relationship may feel like a friendship but it is one-way, with the therapist maintaining a focus on you to help you discover your inner truth. A counselor is not a friend in the usual sense, though you and the professional may grow to care for each other very deeply. A counselor is a true confidant, but not a friend in the way I am talking about friendship here.

FRIENDS FOR LIFE

The traditional wedding vow contains the line "In sickness and in health, for better or worse, until death do us part." Of course many couples delete the lifetime clause, preferring to leave an escape option. And for many marriages that turns out to be a good thing.

When we make a life-long commitment to anything—integrity, good health, spiritual vitality, or a relationship—we have created a foundation in our psychic landscape that we can stand upon as the unexpected challenges of life come our way. When the going gets rough, we hang in there. When the person we are committed to evolves into someone other than whom we had expected, we stay with them to see what will happen next.

I had known about this concept in my own marriage and as a marriage counselor, but until I interviewed Stan about his friendship circles I had never heard the idea applied to friends. Stan told me that he had two long-standing friendships where he had made a conscious decision that regardless of what happened in their lives, he was committed to being their friend for life. He said that decision assured he would reach out frequently to check in and make sure the friendships did not drift away. And he included these two people in his sympathy circle for support when trouble arose.

Holding a friendship for a lifetime takes commitment and hard work.

Sometimes people simply find they have become life-long friends, like Patty and Betty. They knew each other as teenagers, but when all the school functions and boyfriends had drifted into the past they still had each other. They were matron of honor at each other's weddings, they watched each other's kids grow up, and when Betty moved to the other side of the world they stayed in touch. Sometimes it was months between stateside visits, letters, or an occasional expensive overseas phone call. When the Internet technology came along, they were able to use e-mail to connect more often.

One night Patty got a middle-of-the-night call from Betty, who was in a Tokyo hospital. Her husband had just been admitted with a heart attack. Betty's husband recovered, but until he did her bond to Patty was a lifeline. These two women will be lifelong friends because magic dances between them.

Of course unpredictable events come down the pathways of our lives that can derail friendships in spite of our best efforts. Leslie and Shirley were editors in the publishing business who became very close friends over a twenty-five year period. Then a scandal erupted in the publishing house where they both worked. Shirley erroneously believed that Leslie was responsible for the trouble and cut off all contact with her. No matter what Leslie did, Shirley would not let the injury between them be healed. Leslie knew she was the victim of a cruel circumstance and had lost her friend because of it. It was a bitter, painful loss for her. But she decided that they were friends regardless, so she continued to pray for Shirley and her family. In that way she could still hold the connection inside herself and remain faithful to her inner commitment to her friend for life.

A COMMUNITY EVENT AND A PRIVATE AFFAIR

A friendship is also an asset to the surrounding community. If it truly becomes a place for two people to play, challenge each other, give support, and hold each other in the collective heart of the relationship, then the friendship will become a bright, shining presence that everyone can feel. In the same way if two people are in conflict, everyone around is affected. Every heart-filled relationship enriches the community. So to some extent, our friendships are community property because their strength pumps energy into the surrounding human field. And in a similar way, the strength of the community pumps strength into our individual relationships.

Dennis and Gil spoke about how their immersion in a training community set the tone for their open and loving relationship. As Dennis puts it, "We've shared our friendship with many others and they have talked openly about us." He goes on to say, "Many people come to me for therapy because they know that I am capable of having a good male-to-male relationship." Dennis and Gil also talk about how they have become adjunct parents to each other's children, like good uncles. The presence of their friendship has enriched the families and marriages of both men.

> *Friendships are both intensely private and belong to the community.*

And yet a friendship is a private affair, which at some level exists to affirm the two people involved. It may spring from the common ground of work, neighborhood, school, or family, but ultimately it develops its own private ground, rituals, and values. It does not have to report to any parent, employer, or government agency. As long as it does not interfere with other people, it does not have to account to anyone for its activities, beliefs, and delights. It exists totally for the creativity, support, caring, and playfulness it provides. If something productive, like an invention or a new company or a child, comes out of the friendship, that is a bonus not the primary purpose of the bond.

THE DEVELOPMENT OF A TRUE FRIEND

New friendships tend to form when two people are in the same place around some common theme. As long as they continue to walk the same common ground and they both continue to affirm each other, the relationship has a chance to grow into a friendship.

Sometimes it happens that the common ground drops away, but if they value what they have between them, one or both of them can work to create a new common way to be together and continue the affirmation that they both enjoyed. This may be what it takes for them to become faithful old friends.

True friendship has evolved through the issues of jealousy, rivalry, or competition and does not require hiding behind a mask. A true friend has gained your trust by keeping commitments, accepting you as you are rather than for what you can do for him, nudging you along when you need to grow, and canceling important engagements to be with you in time of need.

A friend becomes a faithful old friend when he or she has been around for a long time—has seen you through thick and thin, has stood by you through the years when you have suffered pain and were your most obnoxious self, and has shared in your confidences, fears, and triumphs. A faithful friend will be the one to take you to the nursing home when you are old and infirm, when there is nothing left in it for him except his caring and commitment to your relationship. Dennis and Gil see their friendship as ending on the park bench together as they watch the pigeons. A faithful friend has shared in the flow of your life and somehow understands who you are and loves you just for you.

There are very few of these long-term, deep relationships because they take so much time. Yet they are one of the most precious treasures you will have in your personal village. They are more precious than wealth and fame. These are relationships that will dance you into the grave with a wave of gratitude.

When you start a relationship, you never know if it will skip along on the surface of acquaintanceship or if it will dive deeply into that bonded depth of true friendship. If you treat every relationship with respect and due care, as if it will eventually dive deeply, then a few will actually do exactly that. You never know which of your relationships will turn into a long-term friendship.

Now let's turn our attention to the coterie. A coterie is the group equivalent of a confidant. It is every bit as powerful and rich as a life-long friendship. Both friendships and coteries are rich fields of grokking. I introduced you to this idea earlier, but now we will study coteries in depth.

In Summary

- A true friend is one who is high on the intimacy scale.

- A true friendship has a magical quality about it.

- A true friendship allows both of you to be who you truly are.

- It takes time to develop a true friendship—a lot of time.

- A true friend challenges you to be your best and yet accepts you as you are.

- A confidant helps you hold the weight of life.

- People who have two or three confidants are happier and live more productive lives.

- We can make a lifelong commitment to a select few friends.

- Holding a friendship for a lifetime takes commitment and hard work.

- Friendships are intensely private, yet belong to the community.

- A friend can be one of the most precious treasures in your personal village.

Resources You Can Use

Wind in the Willows by Kenneth Grahame, 1908

> This great children's classic is the story of four friends, Mole, Water Rat, Badger, and Toad. You are in for a treat if you have not read this wonderful, fanciful story about a friendship between four totally different and unlikely characters. It is a rich story about friends accepting each other for who they truly are. It has become one of the classics of children's literature because it holds truths for all of us.

Do I Have to Give Up Me to Be Loved by You? by Jordan and Margaret Paul, 1994

> The central thesis of this very practical book is that if you are not at peace with yourself, you cannot be at peace in a relationship. The authors lay out a clear process of how to get clear, come to peace with yourself, and then take that clarity back into any relationship. A workbook exists under the same name, which will guide you step-by-step toward inner clarity. This is a very useful book for all of us. I strongly recommend it.

The Friendship Book by Rita Robinson, 1992

> A beautiful, heart-filled book about how friends truly stand by each other. It offers clear instructions on how to make friendship work in your life.

The Grateful Dawg, a film documentary about Jerry Garcia and
David Grisman, 2000

> After Jerry Garcia of the Grateful Dead passed away, his
> family pulled together film footage of his musical career
> and his relationship with David Grisman. The resulting
> documentary captures the depth of the friendship between
> these two great musicians. You can actually watch how
> deeply entrained they are on each other as they play. And
> it is filled with wonderful music.

CHAPTER 10

The Cozy Coterie

A coterie is a small group of people who agree to meet regularly to give each other support. These groups are private, intimate, and the group equivalent of a confidant. The coterie has been the base unit of society throughout all of human evolution, and whenever society falters, people will return to the refuge of the coterie to rebuild. It takes much work to become a member of a coterie. There are four ways to establish yourself in a coterie: create one from an existing group, join one that is forming, find your way into an existing coterie, or start your own. The coterie is such a valuable resource that it is in the best interest of everyone to belong to one.

It is 6 AM Wednesday morning. Every week Wayne gathers with six other men for their weekly prayer group. Here they are again, with coffee cups in hand, greeting each other like brothers. For the last seven years they have been praying together for members of the church, a newly wedded couple, family members, world leaders, and for each other. Standing together on a deep faith, they have shared just about everything in their lives: sorrow and delight, disappointment and triumph. When Wayne's wife became seriously ill they prayed for her and came to visit her in the hospital. When

> *Coteries rank very high on the intimacy continuum.*

Wayne retired they listened as he described his relief and his hopes for the future. When his father died they were there.

Over the years this select group of men has grown to know each other in a way that is exquisitely personal and confidential, while at the same time remaining committed to improving the world around them. Their brotherhood is so private that they agreed to tell me their story only if I promised to write it in a way that no one could ever identify them.

This prayer group is a coterie (pronounced *coh-ter-ee*). Like a deep friendship, a coterie is private and intimate. And yet, like a good friendship, this gathering benefits the surrounding community.

Coteries take many forms, but the one thing they all have in common is that they are an assembly of a select few who have made a mutual commitment to gather regularly to give each other support, and often in the process to benefit something larger than themselves. Wayne's coterie came together to participate in the ancient practice of praying together.

Any of the following (to name a few) can become a coterie:
- *A family*
- *A therapy group*
- *A book discussion group*
- *A writers' critique group*
- *A support group of professionals*
- *A women's support group*
- *A prayer group*
- *A weekly quilting group*

Coteries have been around since humans first gathered into close-knit family units and tribes. We are genetically encoded to band together into small intimate groups for support. George Homans, in his classic work *The Human Group*, pointed out that humanity and culture sprang from the small core group, and whenever society or culture falters the small group—the coterie—is where we take refuge as we rebuild.

Although we have been forming them since humanity began, the word *coterie* itself originated with the French word *cot*—meaning hut. Coterie originally referred to the social organization of peasants who lived in huts and farmed land for a feudal lord. The word spread from France to England, and gradually came to refer to an intimate and often exclusive group of people who had some compelling common interest or purpose. In Holland in the seventeenth century, it once referred to that group of people to whom you would give the key to your house.

COTERIE IS A REFUGE

Like the warm embrace of a loving mother, a coterie can provide that emotional place where we give and receive human warmth, settle into a sense of belonging, and feel safe to become who we truly are. A coterie, along with true friends and family, is one of the few places in this unsettled world where we can find solace and a refuge from the stresses of daily life.

In a coterie we have teamed up with compatible people who are committed to being gracious and generous and will hang in there with us when we become cranky from the press of daily life. The presence of others who have known us for a long time is like an emotional salve that soothes our inner state in ways quite mysterious.

Stable membership and commitment by each member to gather frequently and give mutual support is what sets a coterie apart from an ordinary group.

Not all small groups are coteries, but coteries are always small and intimate. They are always multi-stranded, with every individual having a strong significant connection to each member. Stable membership and commitment by each member to gather frequently and give mutual support is what sets a coterie apart from an ordinary group. People do not come and go frequently in coteries like they do in fellowships or groups that are more open. Members tend to stay for a long time.

There are several specialized kinds of small groups that gather around some common ground.

> *Coterie:* A small group of people who make a commitment to meet regularly over an extended period of time to give each other support.
>
> *Clique:* A small group that stresses an often selfish or arrogant exclusiveness. A clique could be described as a group where the primary reason for existing is to exclude others.
>
> *Cabal:* A small, very secretive group that meets to plan and carry out back-room political intrigue or to plan revolutionary or terrorist activities.

It is worth your time to find or develop a coterie. As you know from Chapter 9, research shows that people who have a confidant outside of their primary relationship enjoy more happiness and productivity in life. It is my belief that people who have found their way into a coterie enjoy the same benefit.

Getting into a coterie is more difficult than turning a friend into a confidant. This is because with friendship, only two people are involved. In a coterie the group dynamics, agendas, and schedules have to find a synthesis with the complex issues of several individuals. It will take work and commitment on your part. If you haven't been born into one, there are four ways to establish yourself in a coterie.

CREATE ONE FROM AN EXISTING GROUP

As a serious student of astrology, Valerie hired a private tutor to teach her. They had been meeting every two weeks for a couple of years when the tutor asked if two other students could join them. Then they were four, three students and one teacher. It turned out they were all mothers, some still with small children, others with grandchildren. Another two years went by, and they grew to know each other quite well as they looked at each other's lives through the lens of astrology. Their conversations often turned to personal matters. They celebrated each other's birthdays and helped each other out when one of them had a childcare or medical problem. After about five years they began to realize that what they had was unique, rare, and very, very special. They looked forward to their meetings as a place where they could be stimulated and emotionally nourished. The small study group had evolved into a coterie.

You never know if a group you are involved in will drift toward the kind of commitment, intimacy, and longevity of a coterie. If it starts in that direction, you can take a hand in nudging it along just in case it does turn into that kind of jewel.

How do you nudge a group into a coterie? By making a commitment to come regularly to the group. Keep confidences. Lubricate the workings of the group by holding an attitude of kindness, generosity, and gratitude in all your interactions. And you can encourage others to do the same. Talk up the value of meeting regularly and of holding to a small, exclusive membership. Your input might just be enough to prod the group into a committed coterie.

In the depression of the 1930s, when life was hard and money was in short supply, a group of nine young women gathered together to share resources, sew for their families, and make Christmas and birthday presents for their children. Every Tuesday morning they arrived in each other's homes, sometimes with little children in tow, for sewing and talking.

They called it the Sewing Circle. Over the years they talked about every conceivable part of their lives: money, husbands, church politics, and their private concerns. They shared babysitting, recipes, and produce from their gardens. When World War II came along and some of their husbands went off to war they continued to meet, giving support and solace as they all worried about what would happen next. In time prosperity returned, some were widowed, children grew up, eyesight dimmed, fingers stiffened, and their numbers thinned. They are old and feeble now, and though they no longer sew, those who are left continue to meet for an occasional dinner to enjoy the harvest of a rich life shared with each other.

This small group of women was surrounded by family, neighbors, and the church community, some of whom joined them for picnics and socials, but at the core of this neighborhood circle lived a coterie of women whose shared intimacies and moments were known only to themselves. They did not start out to form a coterie, their group simply evolved into one and, recognizing what they had, they nurtured its life.

Join A Coterie That Is Forming

Sometimes you will have the good fortune to have a small, committed group invite you to join. Bruce and Sally were married by a minister who invited them to join a couples' support group. Intrigued, they were soon the cute newlyweds in a group of couples, some of whom had been married for decades. Everyone made a commitment to meet weekly for ten weeks. They were free to discuss any issue relevant to their lives or their marriages. After the first ten weeks, everyone was so enthusiastic about the experience that they continued to meet for another two years.

In their group they talked about money, in-laws, childcare, sex, and balancing busy family lives. For Bruce and Sally it was a grand initiation into marriage by a group of experienced couples. Eventually the coterie came to an end because their common interests diverged and they began to drift apart. But those two years gave Bruce and Sally a head start on their relationship that paid dividends beyond their wildest imagination.

Sometimes you have the good fortune to be around when a new coterie is forming and you can invite yourself to be a part. James and Grant were colleagues, so as Grant was thinking out loud about starting a coterie James was intrigued, and after talking it over with his wife he asked Grant if the two of them could be included. Grant agreed.

The coterie that Grant had in mind was a writing group for a few compatible couples. They agreed that every person would write something about their lives which they would read to the group. Couples were encouraged not to share their writing with their spouses until the actual group meeting. They gathered once a month to read what they had written and to dialogue about the issues that emerged.

At first the writing was about events in the participants' lives: things not very intimate but interesting. Often the husband or wife was surprised to learn some new dimension of their spouse, which they had not known about before the reading. In time everyone began to know quite a bit about the personal history of each individual. Gradually the level of trust increased, as everyone discovered that what they shared was respected with privacy and trust. The personal sharing became more intimate with each passing month. After about three years the members began to share the kind of material usually found only in a personal journal. This group of five couples became a very significant coterie of friends because of Grant's vision.

By the simple act of inviting himself into an opportunity that was right in front of him, James found a rich resource for his marriage and a whole new circle of friends. The lesson here is to be alert to opportunities when they present themselves to you.

FIND YOUR WAY INTO AN EXISTING COTERIE

Lucille loves opera. Once at a performance she made the acquaintance of a fellow opera buff, Joelle. They struck up a friendship and eventually began to buy tickets together. Joelle belonged to a coterie of fellow opera lovers who met before every new performance to have dinner. Following dinner, they would listen to the opera and then talk about it. Lucille was intrigued and asked Joelle if she could come. Joelle was not sure because it was a very private group that had been meeting for several years, but she agreed to introduce her to some of the group members at the next performance and to put in a good word on Lucille's behalf. The others in the coterie discussed it for quite some time because their membership was very private and precious to them, but in the end they invited Lucille. Now she had a coterie of people who loved good food, wine, and opera, and who shared a very private kind of experience.

You can do this also. If you hear about a coterie you would like to enter, ask one of the members if you can join. Remember that the other members will not take your request lightly. They have spent a lot of time developing trust and mutual caring for each other, and they will not automatically agree to your joining. If you can apply the Principle of Seven with more than one member, you will increase the likelihood that they will take the risk of admitting you into their coterie.

Once you are in the group, be sure to treat what they have created with great respect. This group is a very important and rare resource for each member. Your presence and participation will have to respect and add to that fact. Remember the virtues of kindness and generosity and to respect all confidences. Not only is this coterie a great resource for the other members, it is for you also.

Start Your Own Coterie

Heidi first learned about the power of coterie in a therapy group after she had left a very abusive marriage. Her marriage had deeply injured her spirit, so the healing field of the therapy group was balm to an open wound. That group taught her the power of a coterie and she decided she wanted this kind of resource for the rest of her life. But she did not want to be in therapy forever.

Heidi had two close friends, Rene and Diane, whom she had known since college. She shared with them her desire that they form a study group. For the first couple of years they did not take her suggestion seriously. But eventually the idea began to catch on and they decided to give it a try. Diane knew of a woman, Pauline, whom Diane felt would be a good addition to the group. Heidi and Rene agreed, Pauline was invited, and she accepted.

At Heidi's suggestion, they met at Heidi's house for dinner with the express purpose of discussing how they could make this group work. At this meeting they decided to meet one evening a month for a year and to focus on personal growth issues. They agreed to focus their attention on personal growth books, inspirational tapes, summaries of workshops they had attended, and personal growth exercises that they had learned. After several months Pauline announced that once a month was not enough for her, so they agreed to meet every other Monday evening—first for dinner and then for a focused, two-hour sharing session. The depth of intimacy and trust that eventually grew between them was exactly what Heidi had hoped would happen.

Heidi created a coterie by holding in her mind a steady vision of the kind of group she wanted. She was thoughtful in selecting the members and in setting the tone for how they would spend their time. She encouraged them to hold in confidence what they shared, and she encouraged them to continue to meet regularly. This coterie had been under way for eight years when Heidi described this group to me, and for all I know it is still going on.

This is one way to start your own coterie. Carefully choose the fellow members, set a tone for persistence, provide a focus, and encourage the kind of activities and values that will create staying power. If you want to start such a group, you could share this chapter with the potential members as a guide to getting started.

What do you do if you are new in town and want to start a coterie? Geneva was a woman who pulled up roots and moved halfway across the country. One of the roots she pulled out was to a very supportive coterie. New to town, she set right to work creating a new one. As a group therapist, she understood the principles she would have to apply to create a successful intimate group.

Heidi had developed her coterie out of her already established friendships. Geneva, on the other hand, had moved to a new city and had to start from scratch. When she first moved from Kansas City to Berkeley, she had not taken into account that the large personal village she enjoyed in Kansas City would not come with her. She was shocked by the isolation she felt in her new hometown. No one had ever heard of her in California, so she had trouble finding work in her field as a group therapist. She decided to take a job at a local hospital while she finished her drug and alcohol counselor certification.

In Kansas City her coterie of women had been an anchor point in her life and she wanted that experience again. Geneva developed a plan. She set out to meet as many people as she could, including potential candidates for a new coterie. She actively reached out to her fellow workers in the hospital and to her fellow students in the drug and alcohol program. As she began to develop a circle of acquaintances, she invited some of them for dessert and conversation. This growing circle of women began to meet for dinner and eventually became theater buddies. Several of these new acquaintances became friends. She was quite purposeful about inviting anyone who seemed interested and compatible to every kind of event she could dream up. In addition to having a lot of fun, she was strategic in her search pattern for just the right people for her soon-to-be coterie.

After two years she had a growing circle of friends, five of whom seemed to be good candidates for coterie mates. She invited them to dinner, and over dessert described the coterie of women she had left behind in Kansas City. She proposed that they create one of their own. Four of the women were quite interested, so they began. She had selected her fellow members carefully and the group thrived. Geneva was back home in the embrace of a coterie.

Sometimes people will pull together a coterie to support themselves through a particular project or time in life. Laura teamed up with four other women who were all struggling to complete their Ph.D.s. They formed what they called a "dissertation support group." Meeting weekly to cheer each other on, they agreed they would continue to meet until all five of them had finished their doctorates. They listened to each other complain about their degree committees. They commiserated about the lack of money and the heavy work load. And they shared their doubts that they would ever finish this gigantic project. Together they laughed and cried, talked about their boyfriends, the politics of the university, the scandals in the departments, their hopes for the future, and their doubts. And in the end they toasted each other on the successful completion of their doctorates. They had purposefully created an emotional life raft that would carry them collectively through the rigors of graduate school.

YOUR COTERIE IS A VALUABLE RESOURCE

Most people have only one or at most two coteries at any given moment since a coterie takes so much time and energy to maintain. In fact you can consider yourself lucky if you have had just a few of these groups during your entire life.

Many people go through their lifetimes without knowing the magic of a life-enhancing coterie. Those who are fortunate enough to find themselves wrapped in the embrace of a coterie enjoy an enrichment of life that at times can be amazing to each member. Many professionals know that the key to success for them is to either assemble or to find their way into a coterie that supports their career and provides personal support.

Joe was the director of a big advertising agency. At the top, he felt professionally lonely. He could not confide in his subordinates and he could not confide in fellow directors in the industry either. He realized he needed a support group, so he approached several CEOs of large corporations that were so diverse they had no competitive interest in each other. When Joe proposed they form a group to discuss the kinds of issues that only they faced, several joined eagerly. They made a pact to assist one another and to meet once a month for an extended lunch. A critical part of their pact was total confidentiality about everything they shared. The relief of being with fellow travelers was so great that they began to spend long weekends together at a distant resort. They openly shared the stresses of dealing with competition, regulations, unions, employee problems, and most of all the lonely position of being at the top where everyone either deferred to them or tried to attack their position. By carefully selecting the other members and setting the framework for how they would be together, Joe had created a coterie that was of value to each of these men.

Like these professionals, you can take a proactive approach to finding or creating a supportive coterie for yourself. If you live your life by default, you are trusting to chance that such a rich jewel will come into your life. But if you purposefully go about immersing yourself in a coterie, you will enrich your life beyond measure. It is in your own best interest to surround yourself with a coterie.

Of course very few coteries go on for a lifetime. Most end after a while because people move away or the common ground around which they initially gathered evaporates. Expect your coterie to exist for a period and eventually to end. Then you can use your knowledge to find your way into another one.

We have talked about neighborhoods, salons, fellowships, friendships, and coteries. Now it is time to put this all together and talk about the alternative or intentional family. Those of you who are not embedded in a strong natural family will find the intentional family, which is a cross between a fellowship and a coterie, an especially valuable addition to your personal village.

In Summary

- A coterie is a small group of people who agree to meet regularly to give each other support.

- A coterie is private, personal, and very intimate. It is very high on the intimacy continuum.

- A coterie is the group equivalent of a confidant.

- We are genetically encoded to find support in small groups. The coterie is the most intimate type of small group.

- Whenever society or culture falters, the coterie is where we take refuge to rebuild.

- The coterie is multi-stranded, meaning that each individual is significantly connected to every other member.

- There are four ways to gain entrance into a coterie.
  1. Create one from an existing group.
  2. Join one that is forming.
  3. Find your way into an existing coterie.
  4. Start your own.

- There are five key ingredients to a successful coterie.
  1. Commitment by each member to attend regularly.
  2. Knowledge that confidences will be kept.
  3. Respect for each other as unique individuals.
  4. Being candid in your conversations.
  5. Application of the virtues of kindness and generosity.

Resources You Can Use

The Support Group Sourcebook: What They Are • How You Can Find One • How They Can Help You by Linda Klein, 2000

> This very useful handbook will answer all your questions about how to make your coterie work. If you want an effective coterie, be sure to study this heart-filled work.

Winning with People: Building Lifelong Professional and Personal Success Through the Supporting Cast Principle by Michael Zey Ph.D., 1990

> Zey has pulled together the material that professionals use to set up a group which supports them through a project or a phase in their life. The ideas are rich and stimulating. You will find a wealth of valuable material that will support your efforts to create a successful coterie.

The Human Group by George Homans, 1992

> This is the definitive theoretical book on group theory. If you are a counseling professional who wants to tease your brain, Homans's work will please you no end.

The Divine Secrets of the Ya-Ya Sisterhood a novel by Rebecca Wells, 1996

> A rich and emotional story of four women who made a pact early in life to be faithful friends and to support each other through life's journey. A wonderful story of a coterie of friends who hold to their commitment to support each other through the challenges of the decades. It was made into a very popular movie by the same title.

I Am Sam, a film featuring Sean Penn, Michelle Pfeiffer, and Dakota Fanning, 2001

> This story is about a mentally disabled man who is trying to raise a daughter, but who is challenged by the authorities to give her up because of his incompetence. Surrounding Sam is a classic though somewhat wacky coterie of equally disabled men who support his efforts to raise his daughter. A very sweet story about the collision between love and what is right. Watch how this coterie works and how it supports him during his ordeal. You will be inspired by the love and wisdom expressed in this story.

CHAPTER 11

A Real Family For You

The family is the central hub within which we live our lives. When it is strong, our lives will be strong. The family is the base unit that assures our basic needs are met. It is a resource we need throughout our lives. When the family is weak or thin, we can bring in others to augment our nuclear family. This is called the alternative or intentional family. By being purposeful and applying the principles of good personal village building, each of us can revitalize our family-surround as the ever-changing flow of life sweeps us along from birth to death.

THE FAMILY IS THE CENTER

If you are fortunate enough to be embedded in a strong nuclear family, then your life is blessed. But if you are like many of us who live in a world where the nuclear family is scattered, dysfunctional, far away, or not very relevant to what we are doing, you will need to find an alternative, an intentional family, because the need for family never goes away. You will have to find another way to surround yourself with this human core.

The family is the original personal village. It held us when we were born. It can support us through an entire lifetime. If we are fortunate enough to have a strong family system backing us up, our lives stand a good chance of being very satisfying and full. If, on the other hand, our family is weak or meager or missing, then life may feel like it has a hole in it.

Families are often thought of as child-raising institutions. But it doesn't stop there. As this entire book points out, it takes a village to support each of us through our entire life's journey, and the family is the hub of that village.

Certainly childhood is a major part of family life. For the first twenty years we are children, held in the embrace of a family—hopefully. Then after a short young-adult stint, with the original family standing in the wings, we start our own families and very often children take up another twenty years of life. If all goes according to an ideal plan, our children leave and we have a short moratorium without the responsibilities of childcare. Then weddings and grandchildren come along. So yes, children are very often the center of family life.

But the family does much more. It is a community system just like a fellowship or a coterie. And ideally, all community systems function for one purpose: to meet the basic universal human needs.

As we saw in the Introduction, Abraham Maslow, a great psychologist, first noted that the fulfillment of our universal human needs was the driving force for all of human life.

What are these needs?

The Seven Universal Basic Human Needs

1. *The need for food, shelter, and assurance of physical integrity.*
2. *The need to feel emotionally safe.*
3. *The need to belong.*
4. *The need for regular human warmth and affection.*
5. *The need to be competent with our native skills.*
6. *The need for affirmation for who we are, what we do well.*
7. *The need to be involved with a greater transcendent meaning.*

These needs are not luxuries. It is essential they be met if each individual and the family as a whole are to thrive. When these needs are left wanting, every family member suffers.

Ideally, the family provides for all of these needs at every stage as we struggle with the challenges of life. Any family that is not devoted to providing these will be a family in trouble. Yet problems within families have existed throughout history, and for many people still exist.

Family is centrally important, and yet too often it is a total disaster. The lack of strong family units for many of us creates a need to strike out on our own and to find an alternative: to create an intentional family.

THE INTENTIONAL FAMILY: MAKING YOUR OWN

Some of us are born into families, others have to create them. Family can be any constellation of people living together and functioning as a single household. We consider someone family if they will sacrifice for us in ways most other people would not. Family is the collection of people with whom you gather to celebrate and to whom you turn in an emergency—those you have come to know and trust over time.

An alternative family is a group of people who do not live together but gather often to provide many of the elements of an extended family. The alternative family is a cross between a fellowship and a coterie. An intentional family is a group of people who live together in some form. They are very similar so I will refer to them as if they were interchangeable.

The intentional or alternative family is a blend of your confidants, coterie mates, friends, and neighbors. It meets the needs emerging for you and your loved ones at any particular phase in your life. It can augment an already existing nuclear family or it can provide an alternative for those of us without one. It can be an expanded family for folks whose nuclear family is limited. You can make a purposeful effort to create for yourself the type of family that meets your needs.

ALLISON

Allison found an alternative family through work. There she met Kathleen, and gradually a strong friendship developed between these two women. Kathleen was actively involved in an alternative family, so she invited Allison to attend a gathering. Other people liked her, they invited her back, and within a few months she was considered a member of that group.

In Allison's case it was a matter of being in the right place at the right time. I know it sounds like pure luck that she found an alternative family like this. In reality there was some luck involved, but also lots of effort on her part. Allison was purposeful about accepting invitations to the group gatherings. She openly shared information about herself, and she made it a point to reach out to other group members to help with childcare or advice or a walk. By actively responding to the invitation to join and then actively engaging with the activities of the new circle, she won a place in that alternative family. When holidays came, she had a place to go. When they sprung her a surprise birthday party, she knew she was an insider.

Allison said of this alternative family, "I always felt like an alien in my biological family. I always pretended to be something I was not. Here I don't have to pretend I'm something I'm not. And in this group I'm learning real, practical things that I never learned in my family: things like how to greet someone at the door, how to cook a meal, and how to be a good friend. This feels secure, like my biological family did not." Allison found a family with these people through purposefully reaching out to Kathleen, and then by being receptive to what she found.

SUNDAY COFFEE AT THE HOLLANDS'

It is about 4 PM on Sunday afternoon and the driveway is beginning to fill up with cars. The smell of coffee is strong in the kitchen and the babble of voices and greetings fills the air. Neighbors troop through the hedge, kids come scampering in with noisy fanfare, cakes, pies, and cookies pile up on the kitchen counter. Before long, a noisy, happy gathering of families and friends packs the kitchen and family room. It is Sunday Coffee at the Hollands'.

Alternative family is the antidote for the stressed, isolated nuclear family that too often is cut off without a village.

It all started simply enough many years earlier when Whitney and Bruce, their little children underfoot and the day's chores finished, developed the Sunday ritual of sitting down for the American equivalent of afternoon English tea. It was a little break in the day before dinner was started. Over coffee and juice for the kids, they munched on cookies and sometimes on more elaborate desserts. Not only was it a rest for Mom and Dad, it was an afternoon pick-me-up for the children, with lots of chatter. It became a happy family ritual that they all came to treasure.

Gradually they began to invite friends and neighbors to join them. Over the years the circle of people who knew Sunday Coffee at the Hollands' as an institution grew, and people began to show up from far distances. The conversation around the crowded table was rich and full. Friends brought their children and sometimes their relatives. Neighbors brought family members. Louise, the elderly widow up the street, would often hobble down the drive with her walker. Leslie, a single parent, started bringing her children to give them the experience of a large family. Several singles and friends of friends began showing up. Every week it was a different mix of people, sometimes only four or five, sometimes forty or fifty. They celebrated birthdays and special holidays and welcomed new people into the circle.

The whole thing was pretty loose, yet there was a consistent circle of people who kept showing up. They began to think of themselves as a large extended family. Sometimes they gathered for a special project or to put on a wedding or to celebrate the holidays. The men went hiking and worked on each other's houses. The women went to lunch together and made pilgrimages to the kitchen store. In all, over a hundred people were a part of Sunday Coffee.

Everyone enjoyed it, including the children who grew up in this weekly ritual of the family gathering at the Hollands'. Occasionally they met somewhere else, but Whitney's kitchen was still the central gathering place, somewhat like a private town square.

This alternative family event did not happen by chance. When Whitney and Bruce saw what was developing out of a simple family ritual, they became very purposeful. They knew that families are anchored in place and thrive on rituals. So they made a special effort to offer this event consistently every week. They continually invited people. They suggested celebrations and promoted additional events, like lawn parties and singing fests.

> *Families are anchored to a place and thrive on rituals.*

Bruce and Whitney became an informal clearing house for all the news of the Sunday Coffee group. And in a subtle way they purposely encouraged the group to become multi-stranded.

The members of this gathering began to reach out to each other. When someone was in need, there were always several people who were available to help. It began to take on some of the qualities of a small town, even though the Hollands lived in the middle of a very large city. Many good friendships developed from this simple weekly event, and everyone considered it family.

Sunday Coffee at the Hollands' was an alternative family for a large circle of people. Others recognized what was happening, and eventually several expanded family groups evolved out of this event. Sunday Coffee, at last report, has been going on for over thirty years, and it is said that you can still drop in at the Hollands' on Sunday and the coffee pot will be on.

Alternative family is the antidote for the stressed, isolated nuclear family that too often is going it alone without a village. Anytime you have a gathering of people who support your immediate family life or provide an alternative to it, you have an alternative family. It can take an infinite number of forms.

Sometimes an alternative family is simply two or three families who spend a lot of time together informally and formally. Bonnie and Karen were thrown together during World War II when their husbands were in medical residency and then were shipped overseas to serve as Army doctors. These two mothers were on their own. They provided emotional support to each other during this difficult time and shared meals, childcare, and hand-me-downs. When the husbands returned, an alternative family had already begun. Sophie and Jacob who lived across the street were soon drawn into the circle. These six friends were together for Sunday dinners, holidays, picnics, births, sicknesses, and weddings. Their children grew up knowing each other almost as brothers and sisters. This expanded family stayed together until the end of their lives.

The lesson here is that two women took what was right in front of them to develop an extended family system that supported their lives. Then as time went on, they intentionally created dinner rituals and parties and invited each other to celebrations, birthdays, and holidays.

If you don't have a family and are alone, or if your family is stressed, you can add people to create the kind of family support system you need. Use everything we have covered in this book. Roam, meet people, and develop relationships. Draw in those people who naturally fit into your life and create an assembly that begins to feel like a family.

People tend to form relationships with those who are nearby. So any time you want to find people for any part of your village, including folks to populate your expanded family, just look around you. Being intentional will pay off. Purposefulness will take continual effort, but it will bear great fruit.

Alternative family is usually found with the people who are already nearby.

NEILA

Neila did that. Neila was a single working mother who found herself socially stranded. She was lucky enough to get a Habitat for Humanity house so at least she was in a neighborhood, but initially she did not know anyone there. Her social circle consisted of the people at work, a few other single moms at the day care, and her distant mother. Roaming in her neighborhood she found a retired couple, Edith and Bob, whose own children were raised and far away. Practicing the Principle of Seven Neila succeeded in developing enough of a relationship with them that one day Edith dropped by with a pie. That was Edith's way of signaling that she wanted more. Gradually Bob and Edith became alternative grandparents to her children and a great source of support to Neila.

Neila very intentionally invited Judy, one of the other moms, for tea and dessert. Then came a birthday party with Neila's and Judy's kids and Edith and Bob. An alternative family was under way. Neila kept adding people whom she felt would support both her and her children, and whom she could support as well. Edith and Bob now had some children in their lives, the children had grandparents, Neila had another friend, and the Thanksgiving table was full.

LOUISE AND JODY

When Louise graduated from school, she moved to a new town with her partner, Jody. They found an apartment, but except for the people at work they felt isolated. They gradually became acquainted with another couple, Rachel and Loren, who were in a similar situation. Eventually they decided to share one dinner a week as a way of having some social contact. They alternated cooking every other week. Gradually over the dinner table they came to know more about each other's lives, and as often happens when personal things are shared, a friendship blossomed. The weekly dinners became weekend out-

Intention is the key to creating an expanded family.

ings and birthdays celebrated. Their gathering began to expand as they met new people. An alternative family was evolving. Louise and Jody were starting to grow a personal village in their new city.

FROM PARTIES TO ALTERNATIVE FAMILY

I once pulled together an intentional family in a very strategic and purposeful way. My wife, Peg, and I both had strong nuclear families that were an intimate part of our lives, yet our parents and siblings did not share many of the interests and values that were growing in us. We wanted an additional circle of friends that felt like family.

At the time I was working in a mental health center and was beginning to meet some very interesting and vital people. I developed a plan. Several of these people shared my propensity for play and silliness, so I invited them along with their spouses to a "Come as Your Fantasy" Halloween party. An evening of play behind masks and costumes left these strangers feeling delighted.

Two months later I invited them back for a Christmas party with singing and much cheer. In January I invited them for an evening around the piano, and in March we had a formal dinner complete with china, silver, and candles. Some of the original guests did not seem comfortable, so as the months went by I invited others in their place. In April it was a theater party, in June it was an outing to a lake, and so it went. Once I proposed we all gather hungry, and then go the local supermarket to collectively decide on and impulsively buy our menu. It was quite a scene, with the kids running up and down the aisles and shopping carts brimming with enough food to feed an army.

Back home we cooked this collective meal and laughed over the huge feast that we had created. With full bellies, we read stories to the children and spread out on the living room floor for a slumber party. It was totally zany.

In each case I defined the events and guest list. For a time Peg was upset because none of these people ever invited us to their homes. I encouraged her to be patient, that my plan was still unfolding. Gradually these people began to know each other around the context of the events we all shared. In about eighteen months this group of strangers had grown to enjoy each other's company and to know quite a bit about each other personally. My wife and I now had a core group of close friends who had a shared history, were anchored in one place, our home, and shared a common interest in playing.

For the first year I was the point of initiation and the source of the life for the group. Initially this was a single-stranded group. That is, everyone had a relationship with me but not much with each other as individuals. Gradually the members began to meet each other outside of the playful events that I created. A multi-stranded network of bonds began to develop.

One evening after a theater party, Lois proclaimed that this was as far as the group could go focused only on play. She suggested that we explore the more serious side to our lives. At Lois' initiation, the group agreed to talk about doing something together that was deeper. I had hoped someone would step in, knowing others would have to share the leadership if the group was going to continue. Out of that meeting came a decision to meet weekly for a year, without children, to share dinner and talk about anything that was important. The resulting alternative family became one of the most important centers of support for each of us.

At one point one of the couples in that coterie fell on economic hard times. The rest of us helped with food and gas while they looked for work. The job that finally did come was located by one of the group members. All of us felt more deeply bonded by being able to hold this safety net under two of our members during a hard time. Eventually one couple divorced and two others moved out of the area, so the family came to an end.

Though we no longer meet, the bond between us is still very deep. Now when I run into one of these old family members, it is like being in the company of a dearly loved brother or sister.

As you can see, all the principles and strategies we have covered in this book were applied to create an alternative family system for each of these people: anchoring in one place, following the common ground, hanging out with people who naturally appear in our sphere, applying the Principle of Seven, and being purposeful. You can do the same thing.

BE INTENTIONAL

I cannot emphasize too much the importance of being purposeful about your relationships. Intentionally creating family rituals, fostering trust and safety, and capturing the family history with stories told over and over, to name a few, will enrich any family and create a fertile ground for children to grow. And when an expanded or alternative family is called for, strong intention is the way to assure that it develops.

There is no end to the ways people can be intentional about this. Some people very strategically create intentional families with all the structure and effort used to start a business. Often gay couples will create such a family, even with a written contract, to provide a solid family system in which they can raise children. It is not uncommon for several family units, related or not, to agree to buy houses close to each other in order to create a walk-around type of community situation.

In the 1960s communes became popular as intentional families, and a few of these are still under way. Usually a group of unrelated people would pool their money and buy a house or a farm. They would set up an enterprise where they shared resources and skills and did all the things that a family would do. Most of the time communes required

To create an intentional family, set the place where the family becomes anchored, encourage rituals, apply the Principle of Seven, elicit commitment from each member, play together, and foster trust.

a very strong leader who led the way and provided inspiration. Unfortunately when the leader died or faded out, most of those families also faded.

Communes are not very popular these days. Instead, intentional families have sprung up where the members pool some of their resources to buy into a physical situation, and then set up a very strong and intelligent leadership council that does not depend upon one single charismatic leader. The Songaia community did that.

SONGAIA

Several people shared a vision of an intentional community. Eventually they bought a piece of property with several acres, a house, an old barn, and several outbuildings. They lived together in the rather large house for several years, and eventually they decided they wanted more privacy than the house provided.

So they incorporated and hired an architect and a financial consultant to design a planned co-housing community with separate houses. They secured a loan to build a little village of homes. The result was a condominium association that gave them ownership of their individual homes while everything else was shared. They turned the original house into a common house with a large meeting-dining room, a cozy family room, a playroom for the children, a large commercial kitchen, a commercial-size laundry, and some guest rooms.

To govern the association, they established a well-defined management council where everyone had an opportunity to take responsibility for the life of the community.

Songaia means song of the living earth, and as you might expect, singing is a major activity among this community. Each week they share several meals, taking turns with the cooking, and occasionally on Friday evenings they gather in the living room for stories and singing. Once a month everyone gathers for a house meeting where they discuss the practical details of living together.

And another time during the month they meet in the family room for a sharing circle where they can speak from their hearts about issues of mutual interest.

To wander around this intentional village is a wonderful experience of feeling at home with people who obviously care about each other and are very happily living their lives in the shared context of community. They are an intentional community that came into being and flourishes because of the careful planning and efforts of many people who are devoted to keeping it alive and vital.

Songaia has become one of the models of how to put together a successful intentional co-housing community. You can learn more about them by going to their Web site: *www.songaia.com.*

BEING INTENTIONAL IS THE KEY

We all need some kind of family system throughout our lives. The family is called many things and takes many forms, but unless you are lucky this family system is likely to come into place only because you set your mind to making it happen.

You will have to remain purposeful because regardless of the constellation of people you have at any given time, it is guaranteed to change. And change is hard. So far in this book we have moved from the least intimate to the most intimate of relationships and gatherings. Now we need to go to the most intimate of all—your internal emotional reaction as change sweeps through your life.

IN SUMMARY

- The family is the original Personal Village and remains as the hub of that village throughout life.

- The family is a community system that meets our basic human needs.
    1. Food, shelter, and the assurance of physical integrity.
    2. Emotional safety.
    3. A sense of belonging.
    4. Regular human warmth and affection.
    5. Opportunity to be competent with our native skills.
    6. Affirmation for who we are and what we do well.
    7. Involvement with a greater transcending meaning.

- Intentional family is usually made up of people who are immediately available within roaming distance.

- The immediate family often is not sufficient to meet our needs, so an expanded or alternative family made up of immediate family and close others can be assembled.

- Expanded families can evolve naturally, or they can be assembled with intention.

- All families thrive when they are anchored in place and observe rituals.

- Purposeful intention is a key ingredient in assembling and maintaining an expanded or alternative family.

- All the principles described in this book can be used to assemble an intentional family.

- Intentional communities often involve shared property, a formal leadership structure, and a formal agreement about how to conduct business.

RESOURCES YOU CAN USE

The Intentional Family by William J. Doherty, Ph.D., 1997

Doherty's main thesis is that observing regular rituals is the linchpin of family life. Being intentional about taking meals together, marking bedtimes with the children, creating special regular times for couples, as well as observing holidays and special occasions, is the nourishment that brings life and vitality into any family system. This book applies to nuclear families, single parent families, alternative families, and intentional families. It is a heart-filled, practical book for anyone who wants to enhance family life.

It Takes a Village by Hillary Rodham Clinton, 1996

Clinton gives depth and meaning to the old African proverb that it takes a village to raise a child. Applying it to modern life, she describes fully all the dimensions of family and village life that need attention if children are to thrive. It is full of wisdom and very practical insights.

The Art of Living Single by Michael Broder, Ph.D., 1988

Single life by choice or happenstance has many benefits and offers many challenges. Dealing with loneliness is one of them. Broder takes every issue of single life and offers many in-depth, practical ways to think about and address them. If you are living single, this book will give you many ideas.

Internet Links

If you want to know more about intentional families, search under *intentional family*, *intentional community*, *group living*, *co-housing*, and *shared living*. You will find a wealth of links to Web sites that offer information about communities of every conceivable description.

Anne of Green Gables, a film starring Megan Follows, 1985

Originally a novel by Lucy Maud Montgomery and then filmed as a television series, this wonderful story is about an orphan girl, Anne Shirley, who applied every principle and strategy covered in this book to create for herself a rich family and personal village that enriched the lives of everyone she touched. It is a delightful, well-done film that will touch your heart, and which shows the result of being purposeful and respectful to yourself and to everyone around you.

Chapter 12

Embrace Your Endings

Life is a state of continual change, with endings and new beginnings flowing by all the time. We hold our hearts open when we embrace change and the grief, gratitude, and remembrances that accompany it. If we fail to grieve our losses, our hearts close and we lose our ability to love and to form close relationships. To be good at living, we have to be good at grieving. Our friends too will need support as they embrace their endings. Accepting that all things end and understanding the process of grief allows you not only to support your friends but also to maintain your own ability to bond effectively with others and hold your heart open.

Everything changes. Change always means an ending is happening and a new beginning is under way. Adventures begin and come to an end. Entering kindergarten ends the bliss of being with mother. Graduation ends studenthood. Marriage ends single life. Divorce or death ends marriage. Moving to a new home or city ends the familiar comforts to which we were anchored. Jobs come and go. All friendships end eventually. Loved ones come into our life and leave. Life blossoms and ends.

Judith Viorst, a writer of children's stories and a student of psychoanalysis, calls endings *losses*. She says, "We lose our girlhood to become a mother. We lose our childhood by the responsibilities of adulthood. We lose our children as they fly away. We lose our vitality and strength as we grow old. We lose our good looks and stunning figure and illusions. . . . Losses are a part of life—universal, unavoidable, inexorable. And these losses are necessary because we grow by losing and leaving and letting go."

Several thousand years ago King Solomon recognized how change was a natural part of the pulsation of life. He expressed this understanding when he wrote:

There is a right time for everything.
>*A time to be born — A time to die*
>*A time to plant — A time to harvest*
>*A time to kill — A time to heal*
>*A time to destroy — A time to rebuild*
>*A time to cry — A time to laugh*
>*A time to grieve — A time to dance*
>*A time for scattering stones —A time for gathering stones*
>*A time to hug — A time not to hug*
>*A time to find — A time to lose*
>*A time for keeping — A time for throwing away*
>*A time to tear — A time to repair*
>*A time to be quiet — A time to speak up*
>*A time for loving — A time for hating*
>*A time for war — A time for peace*
>
>Ecclesiastes 3:2-8

The Buddhist tradition teaches that nothing is permanent. The only thing known for sure is that we live and that we die. All else is in a constant state of change. Peace turns into war and war turns into peace. Happiness turns into suffering and suffering turns into serenity. Beginnings and endings are the stuff of life. Each beginning means the end of something else. Sometimes the loss is welcome, like the end of a war, but sometimes the loss is difficult. Only after we learn how to embrace our endings can we fully embrace our life.

As you roam in your personal village you will be challenged constantly to accept endings: of place, people, loved ones, status, health, beauty, and eventually your own life. Dancing with change is one of the core arts for living a successful life. Living a full life in the midst of your personal village takes emotional work. A big part of that work is to grieve what is ending in order to make room for what is new.

As a teenager I bought gasoline for 11 cents a gallon at an ancient Shell station that had not changed much since the days of the Model A. Inside, the old guys in the neighborhood sat around the stove and told stories, while mechanics with dirty rags hanging out of their back pockets changed oil, pumped gas, and put in new head gaskets. I soon became anchored to the smell of tires, gasoline, and oil-soaked wooden floors. It was here that a mechanic welded up my muffler and taught me how to change a fan belt. That old gas station was one of the touchstones in my roamings. It helped to define who I was. It nurtured my soul.

When I graduated from college and left home, I felt a twinge of sadness about leaving my familiar childhood haunts including the Shell station with its familiar smells. But mostly I was excited about my new adventure, so I did not think about what was ending. I was unaware of the importance of embracing my endings in those days.

As I pulled my car away from the curb, with my mother and sister waving goodbye, I noticed out of the corner of my eye that my father—a man to whom I was very close—did not come out to bid me farewell. He was standing in the backyard with his back to me, looking down. It crossed my mind that he was sad but I decided not to think about it. Only later did I learn that I could have marked that ending for both of us in a more compassionate way.

A new city, a new job, marriage, and children. And on the edge of my neighborhood I found an old Texaco station that looked like something out of another era. It was just like the one I grew up with: oil-stained wooden floors in the repair bay, rusty barrels of oil and solvent out back. Inside, the hand-operated cash register was in the corner of a dimly lit office lined with old cans of Stop-Leak and miscellaneous car parts on the shelves. And Morrie was there.

My heart sang. I was back home again. For several years Morrie, who lived in back of the station with his wife, pumped my gas, let me search through the dim corners of his shop for a bolt, and was one of the anchor points in my roamings around the neighborhood. Every week I looked forward to talking briefly with Morrie about the weather or the increasing traffic or the state of his wife's health. Then one day he announced that they had sold the station. I was stunned. Yes, it was time for them to retire. But Morrie was a part of how I defined myself because he had come to represent my connection to my childhood. I had genuinely grown to care for him. The familiar contact with him every week was a predictable experience that brought comfort into my life.

In order to get good at living, we have to get good at grieving.

The last day that Morrie pumped my tank full of gas, I wished him well with a heavy heart. Then I pulled around the corner and allowed myself to cry and cry and cry. Something precious to me was ending and I was embracing that ending with my grief. I lived in the same neighborhood for the next thirty years and every time I drove past the strip mall where Morrie's Texaco station had been, I remembered the warm feelings I'd known in that dark, oily, familiar place. The memory still nourishes me.

By the time I lost Morrie I had learned the profound healing experience that grieving brings. Grieving makes room for the new.

The ability to grieve is one of life's greatest gifts. Embracing grief in the face of loss is a natural and healthy pulsation, like breathing and eating and sleeping. Only when we know how to grieve can we truly love.

Grieving is not easy. But if we resist it, we store up a reservoir of held-back feeling that stifles our emotional expression and interferes with our ability to love and bond to new people and places. In order to get good at living, we have to get good at grieving.

Grieving Is Natural

We don't have to be taught how to grieve. It is one of those God-given gifts that continually allows us to refresh our souls. But we can be taught to bottle up our grief.

Grief is always accompanied by emotion, some of it intensely painful. You will find people who do not want to feel that emotional pain and they make it their business to tell others not to grieve. They do this because others' grief reminds them of their own.

If we buy into their admonition to "stop crying" or "get over it," we lose our birthright. At that point inner renewal stops. Our pathways to aliveness and passion become plugged, and we become subject to depression, anger, physical illness, and even falling out of love. Life can cease to hold vitality. That's when we turn to addictions like television or overwork or drugs or compulsive shopping. That's when we grow tired of the loved ones in our life and go out seeking replacements. Loss of the ability to grieve is a personal tragedy.

What does it take to keep love alive? The ability to grieve!

Why is grieving so important? The answer can be quite complex, but there is also a simple answer. It starts with how you define yourself as a person. The people, events, and situations around you largely shape your inner psychic landscape. Your neighborhood, family, friends, and loved ones help define your inner sense of self. To some extent we are who we are around. We create a psychological mirror of the important people, situations, culture, and physical surroundings outside us. We use this mirror to define how we see ourselves and how we walk in our personal villages.

In addition, as we become connected to others an efficiency develops that allows us to go about our daily business. Others can be counted on to carry out their parts in the complex interactions that make up daily life. For instance, our mother will remind us to put on our shoes in the morning and then point out that we have homework at night. A husband will remember to take the car in for an oil change so his wife does not have to think about it. She will remember that an important insurance payment is due on the first day of June each year so he does not have to hold that in his memory.

Being in tight interaction with others bonds us into a collective memory and efficiency that makes life go smoothly. That is why it is so devastating when a loved one dies or a divorce happens. Our collective memory has been ruptured, and with it a sense of our self.

On top of all this, we humans hunger for bonding in relationship with others. It is in our genetic code. Our body chemistry benefits and our souls sing when we are in the company of loved ones. There is a mystical connection between people who have built a relationship, one that we can feel but which ultimately cannot be described. We all feel it. We need it. Without it, life shrivels.

Endings fracture this mystical connection. The comforting physical and psychological connection we felt with another is torn apart. The collective memory that we have come to depend upon ruptures. And most of all, our inner sense of who we are is seriously jolted. This stirring up inside happens whether we lose a little thing like a neighborhood or a major thing like a dearly beloved spouse.

Felicia and Rick lived together and planned a marriage. Together they held a dream of a nice house with a picket fence and roses, children, and a shared career as physicians. They were deeply in love. Then Rick was killed suddenly in a boating accident. Felicia's entire outer and inner worlds fell apart. For months she cried all the time, lost weight, could not sleep, and walked around in a haze, unable to continue medical school or think about her future and hardly able to feed herself. Her friends stood by and helped as much as they could. A good therapist guided her through her grief so her inner sense of self could reorganize to the point where she could resume her training. It took several years of inner work to heal this inner rupture to her sense of self and of her expectations about what her life would hold. Eventually she was able to create space inside of herself to hold a new relationship, but she always held a special place in her heart for Rick. Felicia was forever changed, and because she had embraced her grief she was able to love again.

Of course death or divorce can be ultimate losses. But every day we suffer all kinds of losses, like breaking a favorite coffee cup in the sink or losing a purse or seeing a friend move to a distant city.

There is more: disappointment. All of us develop an idea about how things are going to be. We grow to expect our loved one to be consistent about remembering birthdays or always to be considerate. Sometimes these expectations come from experience and sometimes they come from wishful thinking. But frequently people change. They disappoint us by not doing what we have come to expect. Because we are attached to things being a certain way, we are disappointed when people don't act the way we expect.

> *Grief is the inevitable price we always pay for intimacy. All relationships end, and the deeper the connection, the deeper the grief at the end.*

Reactions to disappointment are many. Sometimes people simply blow off their inner feelings without facing the fact that they are disappointed. They shut down. Sometimes anger is the result and nasty conflicts can erupt. Sometimes the response to disappointment is revenge. And revenge can take nasty turns, one of them being to totally abandon the person who caused the disappointment and to replace him or her with someone else.

If you have the strength of a Zen Master, you might be able to recognize that your inner expectations are not being met and simply accept it. This is not so easy for most people. Learn to examine disappointment as a call to reevaluate your expectations. When you learn how to do this, you will be more present with yourself and with those around you. Only then can the relationships in your personal village be open and vital and delightful.

Being in relationships with others will always lead to disappointment and loss. Good relationships involve hard work and sometimes have very painful periods. Life with people is a constant process of small, and sometimes large losses, as we refresh our sense of self in an ever-changing world. A rule of thumb: the deeper the relationship has been, the more intense will be the grief at the end. Failure to grieve the loss of an important place or group or person is an insult to the gifts received from the experience.

DOWN THE CORRIDOR AND INTO THE GLOBAL STATE

As you negotiate the pathway of opening to the new, it may help to think of grieving the way that psychologists do. When life or a relationship is going along smoothly and efficiently—with good bonds, a well-developed collective memory, and realistic expectations—it is like traveling down a well-known corridor. Walking that corridor is familiar, comfortable, and easy.

An example of this is when you go every day to the same job on the same bus, have the same tea and lunch rituals with the same people, and banter with your coworkers in the same satisfying way. These familiar rituals make work comfortable and easy. Your inner sense of self and your expectations are all in harmony with the established rhythm.

An end is like walking out of the cozy confines of a corridor into the amphitheater of the infinite.

Then it changes. The company goes out of business or you are transferred to a new division or worse, you are fired. Life in the familiar, easy corridor of work comes to an abrupt end and you are thrown into what the psychologists call the global state. It is a state with no boundaries, no orienting rituals, no defining ways of doing things, and no comforting others. Your inner psychic space opens up from a well-defined space into what seems like disorienting infinite space.

Most people experience this sudden new psychic space as disorienting and become anxious and distressed. Some will try to solve the crisis by resisting the change or leaping into a new corridor or definition, which explains the sometimes crazy behavior people exhibit after a job loss or during a divorce. Some people resort to addictions or become intensely angry, which can lead to domestic violence or rageful behavior. It is a hard time, and it requires great strength to tolerate the sudden loss of structure in one's inner and outer life.

> _The global state is a place with no boundaries, no orienting rituals, no defining ways of doing things, and no comforting others._

If you can recognize that you have been thrust from a familiar state into the global state, however, and if you can tolerate the unknown, a new unfolding will gradually come into view and life will go on. If you can hold on through this period, the new form will be a stronger you with a deeper connection to your native talents and interests. The old adage that time heals is referring to this process.

DIFFERENT ENDINGS—DIFFERENT RESPONSES

Endings are often happy events, and celebrations work to reorient our inner sense of self to the new reality. Leaving single life for marriage is one such time. All the complex arrangements and the marriage ceremony itself acknowledge the end of singlehood and launch us into the next step of a relationship.

We are drawn to punctuate endings in a formal way. When a child is killed along the road, people bring flowers and balloons to mark the place. Afterward a plaque honors the event. In this way the community contributes energy to marking the ending with an outpouring of tears and candles, and perhaps also angry letters to some civic official. We attend funerals as communal recognition of a death. Collectively we acknowledge major endings.

In divorce, the ending is often marked with counseling sessions and lawyers, and sometimes even highly emotional dramas in court. Failure to face our grief over the loss of a marriage can result in nasty public spectacles. By contrast, a very few enlightened people mark the end of a marriage with a divorce ceremony to honor what is ending and to make room for the beginnings to come.

Robert Carlson is a social worker and former pastor who has created a marriage-ending ceremony. He begins by bringing the couple and, if they want, their close mutual friends into a neutral, quiet, calm setting. He asks the couple to bring any significant symbols with them, which are then placed before them. Then he rings a bell and calls for a five-minute meditation. The following Divorce Vows are then pronounced, either together or in turn.

May the love and good things we shared endure and blossom.

May the results of our struggles compost into new growth.

(Number) years ago I embraced you as my marriage partner and life mate.

Now I release you as my marriage partner and life mate.

I honor you as my special companion in the dharma (destiny). May we be loving friends forever.

May we cherish and honor each other and strive to use right speech with one another.

May the blessing of our relationship, past and present and future, benefit our children, families, friends, and community.

At this point Robert rings the bell again and invites everyone present to express thanks, gratitude, and appreciation for what did happen around the relationship.

They close by each walking away in separate directions to signify the ending.

In this way the couple and their friends have an opportunity to gracefully restructure their relationship and their inner sense of self, which had been defined by the relationship. Much of the grief process is very intimate and private. But to have public acknowledgment of an ending, other than a funeral, is an essential part of the process.

Sometimes when we have a pool of unresolved grief from an earlier loss in life, the experience of supporting and grieving with someone else allows our own pool of grief to drain out a little bit. That is why people find themselves crying very deeply over another person's loss.

It seemed that the world collectively grieved the death of Princess Diana, and the global community became a little more alive in the crying. When you stand by a friend who is working through a loss, you help her and you help yourself.

Sometimes an ending is a minor event, like replacing a beloved old car or moving to a new neighborhood. The inner work—grief, if you will—may be no more serious than a faint longing or a brief heavy feeling. When you end something that has seriously defined you in a major way, however, the reorganization work is much more involved.

Cheryl and Sherman had been very happily married for thirty years when he developed a brain tumor. Over a period of ten years he gradually went downhill, still able to live at home for several years but eventually sleeping all the time in a nursing home. At first Cheryl was devastated by what all this meant, but very slowly she began to develop a parallel and then separate life, while her beloved slowly and painlessly slipped away. When Sherman finally died of a stroke, she had almost totally reorganized herself from a married woman to a single woman with many friends and grandchildren. The grief at the end included some tears and some heavy moments, but in general the end was a relief for everyone. Cheryl's journey down the corridor into the global state and back into reorganization was so gradual that, though it was hard, she was not blown away by the experience.

Nancy and Lucille were the closest of friends. They talked every day, shared every confidence, went shopping, shared childcare, skied together, knew each other's lives and families intimately, and for fifteen years forged a bond that seemed like it would last a lifetime.

Then Nancy's friend Patricia became acquainted with Lucille and her family. Eventually Patricia had an affair with Lucille's husband. Lucille was enraged and turned her fury onto Nancy for bringing Patricia into their life. A deep, unforgiving, blaming place opened up in Lucille. She abruptly cut off from Nancy.

Now Nancy no longer had her friendship with Lucille as an organizing principle in her life. She was thrust into the global state of agony, anxiety, and disorientation. Gone were the daily rituals she and Lucille had enjoyed. Gone were the frequent phone calls. Gone was the touchstone of Lucille's kitchen and family. Gone were the happy times on the ski slope. Nancy was totally lost. Fortunately she had her own family and many acquaintances. For months Nancy felt like the rug had been pulled out from under her. She felt like she had lost her only friend.

As she talked about it with her husband, cried, and expressed her sense of betrayal, she gradually began to explore a new friendship, and after a couple of years she was over Lucille, mostly. Two new close friends gradually came into Nancy's life, and now when she thinks of Lucille her feelings are mostly neutral and a little puzzled. Nancy had done her grief work.

Supporting Friends Who Are Suffering Loss

Elizabeth Kubler-Ross wrote the first definitive description of the grieving process. She broke it into five stages, though in reality it is not usually so clear-cut as these discrete steps might imply, and the sequence of the stages can be quite mixed up. Grief is difficult and often chaotic.

The Five Stages of Grief

1. *Denial: This is not happening.*
2. *Anger or Resentment: Someone is to blame.*
3. *Bargaining: Oh God, I will do anything if you will make this go away.*
4. *Depression: I can't function. Life has no meaning.*
5. *Acceptance: It is not easy, but I can go on now.*

When you have a loss, either large or small, you will find yourself negotiating through these stages in some form. Your friends will face losses too, and you will want to be there to support them. How do you do this? For starters, it helps to recognize that everyone travels these same steps through the grief process. How you respond will depend on where your friend is on the journey. Let's talk briefly about these steps.

For example, say your friend just lost a loved one or his house burned down. The first thing you can expect from your friend is that he will be in a state of shock, disbelief, and numbness. This is nature's way of dropping a veil of quiet over the person so he will not be overwhelmed by the loss. He will be unable to process the meaning of what just happened. You can support him during this early phase by simply standing by. He cannot yet take in the concept that a major part of his inner life, not to mention his outer life, has been uprooted. Your simple presence, offering whatever practical support you can—perhaps making a phone call or asking for details about what happened—will be very valuable.

How best to respond to your friend's grief will depend on where he or she is in the journey.

During this period you can provide practical help, like driving somewhere or getting food. If your friend wants to talk, let him say what he wants without trying to cheer him up. Being realistic about the loss is the most important gift you can offer. Listen while he tells you every detail about what happened. That way he can begin to take in the idea that the loss really happened, which begins the internal reorganization process.

As the numbness begins to lift, your friend may become angry and blaming. He will blame himself, the one who was lost, the doctors, the police, the media, anyone he can think of. He may even turn his anger onto you. Here you help by simply listening and not taking sides or joining in the anger or blame. Don't try to talk him out of what he is saying. If he says he is going to get a lawyer and sue someone, simply listen and, if necessary, point out there will be plenty of time for that.

If you are not careful you can become polarized with your friend in his anger and take sides. You might be tempted to join his efforts to punish an abandoning spouse, to take a tirade to the city council, or to march off on a revengeful legal action. Be careful not to become polarized. If you need to take action on your friend's behalf, be careful and realistic. Otherwise your piggybacked anger may only inflame the situation unnecessarily.

As your friend seriously begins to integrate the loss and the massive changes that are going on inside, he will cry, be angry, laugh, cry again, be numb, propose stupid things like taking a lover or getting revenge, cry again, act normal, walk around like a zombie, and ask over and over, Why? Your task here is simply to listen, encourage him to talk about what happened, propose a walk, or gently cool his heels if he starts to launch out on something outrageous. Take your friend to a movie or fix dinner together. Do things that you have done before, like having lunch at a familiar restaurant, going to the theater, visiting friends, anything you can think of that was a part of normal life before the loss. Stepping back on the ground of the familiar, even for short periods, will help your friend come back into an inner harmony that allows his inner equipoise to return.

As your friend recovers, encourage him to resume his old activities, talk about the loss, remember the positive things, look at pictures, and laugh about old memories. With your continued support, sometimes over years, he will reorganize his inner sense of who he is and life will go on.

If the loss to your friend was someone very close, this process can go on for a year, or two or three. If the loss was less significant you might see the process run its course in a few minutes or days.

Crying, talking, remembering, feeling like a lead weight is in the stomach, not sleeping, asking why, being angry, wanting revenge, and blaming oneself are all part of the grief process. When you or your friend can fully embrace all of these things as necessary rather than judging them, inner work is going on and healing is happening. Wisdom is building. Strength is returning. It is not an easy task, but allowing yourself to grieve and supporting your friends through the grieving process is the stuff of life.

WHAT ELSE HELPS?

Loss cannot be avoided. Friends will fade away. Jobs will be lost. Children will move away from home. Loved ones will die. The vitality of youth will fade. Luckily, there are some things we can do to ease the way.

For starters, if you have succeeded in keeping your personal village diversified, you will be in a much better place to make the transit across this loss.

If you have all your people in one basket—job, relationship, activities—when it ends, you are left with a huge hole inside and in your life. The global state will become overwhelming. If you make it a policy to have many relationships at all levels of the intimacy scale, to engage in many activities, and to roam freely and widely, then when one of your supports goes away you'll have a foundation of many people that upholds you during the grief process and the ensuing reintegration.

A strong diversified personal village is your best support during times of change and loss.

-231-

Make it a habit to develop relationships with people both older and younger than you. Then you can be a support to people across the spectrum of life, and they will be the same to you.

Refugees, people who have been uprooted from everything in their lives as they fled some tragedy, often leave absolutely everything behind. Even though they may have had a balanced life in their former world, to lose everything propels them into a global state that often is totally overwhelming. The massive reorganization required is sometimes more than can be managed. Some never do recover. Most of us are not refugees in the total sense of the word, though at times we all may feel like refugees. The extreme scenario of being a refugee reinforces the importance of nurturing a rich treasure chest of people and resources in our personal village. We can draw on that social capital during a loss and be able to find comfort and people to help us build a bridge over the crisis and into a new healthy state.

When You See It Coming

Sometimes we know a loss is coming. If we can celebrate by saying goodbye or doing a farewell ceremony, the grief will not be as bad. These principles even apply to the loss of a pet. Rudy was a much-loved dachshund. He remembered everyone he had ever met. As he reached the end of his life and faced a serious terminal illness, all his family and his old friends gathered to say goodbye. They held him in their laps, fed him sweets, petted him, and let him kiss them like always. Rudy loved the attention and his family felt they were giving him a great send-off. The next day when he was put to sleep, everyone felt a depth of gratitude for him and the joy his antics had brought into their life. Even though everyone missed his bouncing walk and his silly, laughable barking, the loss was softened. If a pet is a central figure in your life, to celebrate the ending of life with them, if possible, will ease the grief.

Gratitude for what you have received is an important dimension of easing loss. All of us have enjoyed an abundance of joy and pleasure, and probably many immeasurable benefits, from whom or what we are losing. Our lives are fuller when we acknowledge the gifts we have received. If you know the loss is coming and can express your gratitude, the reorganization afterward is richer.

When people are faced with the loss of a dearly loved one, it is common for them to drop many of their busy daily activities and begin to shower attention on the one who is about to leave. It always seemed strange to me that people waited until the end to express their affection and gratitude. I once had a cat whom I decided to treat with great affection and attention every day as if it were to be the last. Of course I had a very happy cat on my hands and my heart sang in the process. (Lest you think I only do this with cats, let me assure you that I make it a practice to treat everyone I know in the same way.) When the cat finally had a stroke and died eleven years later, I did not feel grief at her passing. I missed our daily time together and the sweetness between us but there was no sorrow, only gratitude for what we had shared.

Treating everyone with graciousness, warmth, caring, and gratitude is the best way to live in the company of others and to ease the passing when the end does come.

There will be times when we leave a place to which we have grown especially attached. One way to acknowledge the ending is to spend some time in that space and remember what happened there. You can even thank the space. Phyllis is a psychotherapist who describes leaving an office where over a decade of memories were stored up. Before she locked the door for the last time, she spent an hour remembering many of the events and feelings that she had experienced in that office. Many tears had been shed in that room. Much laughter had reverberated from the walls over the years. Often sheer horror had filled her heart as she listened to the stories of the people who came to see her. She thanked the people as she remembered them and thanked the walls for holding everyone through a grand adventure of personal growth. As she went over all of the memories associated with that room, she was able to say goodbye to the office and move on to her new place. The hour she spent remembering helped to reorient her sense of self toward what lay ahead while honoring what was ending.

As mentioned in Chapter 3, research shows that when people are going through major transitions in their lives, it is the people on the edges of their intimate circles who may have resources to offer that are quite valuable. April was going through a nasty divorce but had not been able to find a good attorney. She shared her difficulty with her hairdresser, Angelo. Angelo thought his brother knew a good lawyer and called him on her behalf. The brother called April and soon she had the legal help she needed. April's unlikely connection to her hairdresser that had opened up this resource is common in the loose network of our personal villages. When a major transition, loss, or change is happening to you, be open to ideas and people you do not ordinarily think of as resources. Often you will find help your inner circle does not know about.

If you are so totally overwhelmed with the immensity of a loss that you cannot function, it may be time to think about professional help. If the grief turns into chronic depression or anger, or if it seems to go on and on without ending, this may mean that something deep in your psychological structure has been jarred loose and the restructuring is beyond what you or your friends can handle. This is when a professional can help. A counselor is trained to understand the process and can be very helpful. In severe loss, the help of a support group can be valuable. The company of others who have suffered losses and who are sharing in the restructuring process is often a godsend.

Grief's expression can run the gamut from racking sobs to a solemn inner state. It can be raging anger or a simple acceptance that you need to go on. It can be mind-deadening numbness or a quiet heaviness. We experience inner work in many ways, but regardless of the way it manifests itself and regardless of whether it takes a few minutes or a few years, we all must go through it over and over if we are to be fully alive to ourselves and to those around us.

Once while walking through a cemetery, George came across a man standing stoop-shouldered next to a new grave. He walked up to him and asked gently, "Your wife?" The old man nodded.

"How long were you married?" George asked.

"Sixty-three years," he managed to say.

George nodded. The old man looked down and George walked on. Sadness filled the air. Tears flowed as George realized that one day either he or his wife would be standing by a grave just like that. Grief is the price we will eventually pay for the intimacy we enjoy today. It is a price we would rather not pay, but we know it is the unenviable counterpoint to the great sweetness we experience now.

Knowing how to survive the grief process and how to transform endings into new beginnings is one of the marks of maturity. We can take the gifts that our cherished loved ones have bestowed upon us by letting go when the relationships end. By taking these gifts forward, we can avoid letting the end drag us into depression and withdrawal. Anything less is an insult to the quality of the contact we once enjoyed together.

Life is hard work, and life is change. On the journey from birth to death, the supportive cast of a strong personal village makes this hard work possible and carries us through the continually changing landscape of our lives.

A Chinese emperor once asked his wise men for a statement that would always be true, no matter where, when, or how. Their answer was, "And this too shall pass."

In Summary

- Life is a continual process of change: endings and beginnings.

- Only after we learn how to embrace our endings can we embrace life.

- Knowing how to grieve is a part of the process of endings. When you know how to grieve, then you can truly love.

- Grieving is a natural process, like breathing and sleeping.

- The five classic stages in grieving are:
    1. Denial
    2. Anger or Resentment
    3. Bargaining
    4. Depression
    5. Acceptance

- When you go through the process of grief, you re-organize your relationship to the outer world and to your inner sense of self.

- A sudden loss is like being thrust into zero gravity with nothing to orient you. It can lead to great disorientation and anxiety. When you learn to stay with the resulting anxiety this state produces, then a new reality can slowly emerge.

- Some endings are marked with celebrations and happy congratulations.

- Marking endings with symbols of remembrance, memorials, services or celebrations help to carry us forward into the future while retaining the value of what ended.

- Your friends will need support as they grieve or celebrate their endings.

- You can hedge against total devastation when faced with loss by doing the following:
  - Allow yourself to grieve when a loss occurs.
  - Keep a large, diversified circle of people active in your life.
  - Maintain a life-long habit of revitalizing your personal village by constantly bringing new people into your fold.
  - Reach out to people on the edge of your intimacy continuum during times of change.
  - Maintain an attitude of gratitude for what you are receiving. Let people know you care for them all along the journey. Then when they are gone, you will feel fuller in your heart.
  - Know that every ending marks a new beginning.

Resources You Can Use

How to Survive the Loss of a Love by Harold Bloomfield, M.D., Melba Colgrove, Ph.D., and Peter McWilliams, 2000

> If you need inspiration and guidance to help yourself through the loss of a dearly loved one, this book will very gently and carefully lead you through every question and step you need. It is practical, loving, poetic, and comprehensive.

Crazy Time: Surviving Divorce and Building a New Life by Abigail Trafford, 1992

> Many good books have been written to help guide people through a divorce. This is my favorite. It assumes divorce is a given and will not try to talk you out of it. Many people have walked this well-known, painful path, and this book will describe what to expect and how to make the transit across each step. This is an excellent book for both parties in a divorce to have as a resource.

Transitions: Making Sense of Life's Changes by William Bridges, 1980

> This timeless book describes the process of coping with the difficult, painful, and confusing times associated with changes in life. It is filled with wisdom and practical steps about how to move through the confusion and anxiety into a new sense of yourself. I strongly recommend it if you are going through any major change.

Healing Conversations: What to Say When You Don't Know What to Say by Nance Guilmartin, 2002

> Guilmartin has done an excellent job of showing us how to talk with and comfort a friend who is going through a difficult time. It is filled with caring, warmth, and great wisdom.

The Tibetan Book of Living and Dying by Sogyal Rinpoche, 1992

> I believe this magnificent text about the Buddhist approach to life and death is destined to become one of the classics of modern literature. Sogyal Rinpoche describes in detail the Buddhist approach to change, to the process of death, and to helping a beloved person who has just died. In fact if you recently had a close loved one die, run right out and buy this book, and go directly to Chapter 13. You will learn exactly what to do.

Necessary Losses by Judith Viorst, 1986

> Viorst was a writer of children's stories before she studied psychoanalysis and learned about the psychological journey through life. With the wonderful voice of a polished writer and the wisdom of the ages, she will walk you through all the losses everyone faces in living a full life. This delightful and informative book puts into clear perspective the ebb and flow of change in ordinary life.

Pay It Forward, a film featuring Kevin Spacey, Helen Hunt, and Haley Joel Osment, 2000

> A wonderful, heart-filled film about a boy who discovers that the way to pay back a gift is to pass it on to another person. This simple yet powerful story conveys the very heart of gratitude. It will make you cry. It will make you think. It will stay with you.

Mostly Martha, a German film Starring Martina Gedeck, 2002

> A totally delightful story about a chef named Martha for whom life revolved around fine food. As the story unfolds she is confronted over and over with one change after another, and in the end she becomes more full as a person. It will make you laugh, cry, and salivate from visions of magnificent food, and it will leave you with a warm feeling about a real life being lived fully through all the changes that each of us have to face.

CHAPTER *13*

Now It Is Up To You And Me

For over a century serious thinkers have been warning that the advent of large social, economic, and technological systems is eroding the quality of life for the individual. They all point to the need to restore a strong sense of humanity at the personal and local levels to counterbalance the trends on our planet toward macro, globalized, and big systems. Failure to do so may have dire consequences for us all. One answer is for each person to take it upon himself or herself to create as much vitality and life as possible at the local level, with close loved ones, with local businesses, and in the immediate community.

The tag line *think globally, act locally* is only partly correct. In reality, we have to keep a global perspective while at the same time both thinking and acting locally. Global includes everything outside your roaming-around territory—which may be very small. A teenager's roaming territory may be just the family, the high school, and the neighborhood. Or it might be very large if you roam across nations and continents, either physically or electronically. Whether your territory is small or vast, you have the most impact for yourself and for others when you are close to home. When you start to move out of your roaming space, your potency quickly begins to decrease. *Local* is not necessarily a place. Local means the realm where people have an emotional connection to each other, the realm where people mean something to you personally. Sometimes this emotional connection is very thin, as with the mechanic, the doctor, or the familiar stranger at the bus stop, but it does exist. Your personal village is a local event.

What happens to the people in our roaming sphere is very important. We evolved from a tribal environment and that is where we feel most comfortable and potent. You and I are most at home with the people we know personally.

Yet with the advent of civilization and larger social structures, individuals often become lost and separated from their important people. As cultural systems become larger and more complex, we began to see an evolution from barter and trade to large capitalistic markets. And as capitalism becomes more complex, so does technology. They go hand in hand. Each seems to feed the other.

Now we are facing titanic waves of change, as capitalism and technology sweep over the old tribal systems that still define a good part of the world. Globalization, capitalism, and technology are touted as a good thing for everyone on the planet. And maybe they are. But some of you, and many others, have been raising questions.

In the middle 1800s Germany evolved into a capitalistic society. Many of the great philosophers of the era watched this turn of events with interest and sometimes alarm. Ferdinand Tonnies, in his book *Community and Society*, claimed in 1887 that capitalism destroys community and replaces it with society. By this he meant that community is a system where people relate to each other as individuals, and where interactions and trade tend to be quite personal. In society, people shift this relationship to products and mediums of exchange like money. People are valued more as producer-consumer units than as individuals. The benefits of a consumer-oriented market delight us with products, services, and opportunities never before available. Now you and I can take vacations halfway around the world, drive in air-conditioned comfort to the store or to distant places, and eat food from anywhere on the planet. But the importance of people-to-people relationships is deemphasized.

Capitalism and technology have risen up as grand, sparkling specters, and the value they have brought has been enormous. None of us wants to give up their benefits to our standard of living, life span, medical care, and education. But as society becomes stronger, community often becomes shredded, or at least pushed aside.

In the 1930s interest in sustaining small personal communities was very high, amid dire warnings from the sociologists of the day that failure to do so would cause great social problems in the future. Jacob Moreno M.D., a noted psychiatrist of the time, warned in his 1934 book *Who Shall Survive* that if we did not find a way to establish a strong sense of community for every person, society would begin to unravel. Seventy years later our society is showing signs of unraveling just as he predicted. Terrorism, epidemics of violence and child pornography, massive prison populations, urban sprawl, disaffected youth, teen suicide, and a divorce rate that is a tragedy for our children are just the tip of the iceberg. Events like the Littleton High School massacre are the natural outcome of too many people feeling isolated and overwhelmed.

Today the alarm bells are still being sounded. David Korten, in his 2001 book *When Corporations Rule the World,* points out that the law empowers corporations to make a profit without any consideration for the price paid by people, communities, or the environment. Corporate law protects the investors' right to make a profit—period. As corporations grow they often assume such large dimensions that the people, resources, and communities they touch seem not to exist. What does exist is the continual maneuvering to maximize profits. And the best profits are seen when companies can take on global dimensions, where the best leverage for financial return is to be found.

Korten documents in horrifying clarity the impact that some of these profit-making machines have on individual people, their families, their communities, and the environment all over the world. He and all of us recognize that capitalism in moderation is a good thing, but taken to profit-driven extremes it dehumanizes too many people, sometimes in ways not even recognized.

Workers are too often paid minimum wage, and any profits that accrue are immediately sent out of the community and into world financial markets. Our communities have become like the gold fields in California where miners sluiced away the countryside to unearth the gold, which they took away, leaving behind a landscape that was torn up beyond repair. Some from far away became rich, at tremendous cost to the environment.

One of Korten's answers is to start a countermovement toward valuing what's local. He encourages the enactment of laws that protect the local environment, our resources, and the rights of local people to enjoy a living wage. He encourages individuals to avoid the massive corporate merchandising machines and instead trade with local merchants who make their living in our local communities. Korten acknowledges that you may pay a little more for products and services when you take your business to your neighbors, but the improved quality of life for everyone will more than compensate for what you might save at a big corporate sales outlet.

The contemporary social theorist August T. Jaccaci developed a way to examine the evolutionary process of any living system. His work, in concert with Susan B. Gault, is described in their 2001 book *CEO: Chief Evolutionary Officer*, which applies to such diverse systems as colonies of bacteria, forests, businesses, civilizations, and the entire human family. Jaccaci says that every living system follows a pattern that gradually evolves to higher and higher levels of organization and sophistication. This pattern is predictable in form and occurs on a timescale that can be mapped out. If a system fails to evolve to the next higher form in the allotted time span it will stagnate; it may drop back to an earlier stage of evolution or a sudden destruction may occur. Nature wants living systems to evolve toward higher and higher levels of organization. When Jaccaci maps out this pattern for modern civilization, some very interesting things emerge.

His work shows that it took hundreds of thousands of years for humanity to stabilize the food supply so famine and starvation were less likely to occur. Then it took many thousands of years more for us to learn how to multiply our physical abilities—first with levers, then wheels, and now with bulldozers. It took only a very few thousand years for written language to evolve, first on clay tablets and eventually into the books we use today. The ability to communicate over distances took only a couple hundred years to evolve. And now with computers our new ability to develop and manage complex systems has taken only about fifty years. Jaccaci claims this all follows his theory very well. The story of human civilization thus far shows that we have developed ways to meet all the physical requirements for the human family. The next step in our evolution is love. Jaccaci believes that well-functioning communities are necessary to bring love onto the human stage.

During a private conversation in 2000, Jaccaci told me that the time span for each step up the evolutionary ladder has been cut in half with each advance. His theory indicates that we have about 20 years to bring love into its proper place in the human drama. If we fail to do this in this time period, we run the risk of stagnating or, more probably, moving backward into a more disorganized state, either gradually or abruptly. His work caused him a sense of alarm, and it alarmed me too.

According to Jaccaci we have only a short time to pull community systems into place that will assure love and emotional integrity for everyone on the planet. If he is right, then we'd better get cracking.

Corporations will continue to grow and capitalism will continue to flourish as traders move assets around like pieces on a game board, and the individual will continue to become less and less significant to the system. The evolutionary task for you is to find a way to remain balanced as this huge, global juggernaut lumbers along. Your answer is to develop a strong bond to your local community, your roaming sphere, and the people you know in your personal village.

Too much is written about how to make money and be successful. Too little is written about how to strengthen our personal communities. To fill this void I have written the book you have just read. And that is why I have started the Personal Village project. This money-technology-information driven world has not found many ways to make a profit by encouraging people to band together informally into personal communities. In our profit-driven culture, for all intents and purposes, the ideas of coterie and personal village and grokking do not exist. This means that each of us will have to educate ourselves about this dimension of our lives and take action on our own.

None of us wants to give up the benefits of modern technology and civilization. The leap forward and the promise of more to come is too good. What we all need to do is balance what we have developed with strong communal systems. The ancients understood this, and many, many people today also understand this wisdom. Our task is to bring forth the old wisdom about community so it stands beside and complements our technical, capitalistic, and governmental systems. The place to start is with each of us nurturing the garden of our own individual personal villages.

While you are creating strength in your personal sphere, do remember that we each have a responsibility to bring our energy to bear on community structures at a civic level. It will not be enough simply to retreat from the world and have a cozy personal village. If all of us did that, the world would fall apart and we would be back in the jungles. It is imperative that each of us balance our personal endeavors by voting, becoming active in politics, civic affairs, governmental planning, and by fostering better schools, urban environments, and decent lives for every person on the planet.

This is urgent business. It is up to you and me to create for ourselves, our loved ones, and our neighbors a strong center of love and respect and prosperity. It is up to each of you to become proactive in strengthening your personal villages. Your loved ones and neighbors are counting on your success. Do not leave this effort to someone else. We cannot wait any longer.

The fate of our lives and the fate of the planet lie in our hands.

EPILOGUE

The African proverb that it takes a village to raise a child is well known. But no one knows where this saying came from. It seems to have arisen out of the experience of countless generations of people living together, and it has become part of a verbal tradition whose origin is lost in antiquity. Yet it is true that childcare is a huge job which requires the efforts of a whole host of people to shepherd each one of us from the womb into adulthood.

In Africa and in other less technically-oriented cultures, people also know that it takes a village to support us along the journey from birth to death. Villages are not just for children. Villages are small gatherings of people who all know each other and, in one way or another, give each other support on life's journey. We need each other. We always have and always will.

We humans are magnificent. The range of possibilities for us seems to be endless, and the opportunities for individual greatness are beyond imagination. By greatness, I am not talking about fame. When a mother cares for her child, that is greatness. When a song is sung, that is greatness. When a flower garden is planted, that is greatness. When a sunset is watched, that is greatness. And yes, we have difficulties too. From the greatest to the most difficult time, we need each other: our personal villages.

When Laurens van der Post, an English gentlemen, world traveler, and adventurer, studied the Bushman in Southern Africa in the early 1900s, he learned their language and wrote extensively about their life. The folks there grew to know him; so one day when he was walking through the countryside, he was surprised when a Bushman emerged out of the brush and greeted him with something like, "Oh, hello Laurens. Before you came I was dead, but now that you are here I am alive."

Such a bizarre statement. What did the man mean by this strange greeting? My thought is that this culture knew that when we are alone we are not fully alive, but in the company of those we know we are alive in every way. His greeting acknowledges the importance of being with others and the importance he placed on his relationship with Laurens.

Social scientists and neurobiologists have given us the good news: hard evidence exists that we thrive when we are with one another. And these scientists also give us great language to describe that state: limbic resonance, attachment, interdependence, entrainment, and bonding. Poets, lovers, and parents have always known this, and these people simply use the word *love* to describe what is going on. *Love* is one of those words we all know about but cannot define, or which we have reduced to a simple tag line. It exists in our hearts. And "holding something in your heart" is also one of those phrases that we all know about but again, it is a phrase that defies a clear definition.

I hold my love for God in my heart. I hold my family in my heart. I hold my friends in my heart. I hold my life-mission in my heart. It seems to be a part of our humanity to know what that means. Even little children know about it as soon as they learn how to speak.

Once while visiting some friends in Kenai, Alaska, I was having an engaging conversation about fishing, when I looked over at Julie who, with that three-year-old's twinkle in her eyes, looked up at me and, tapping her chest with her fingers, said out of the blue, "My family is in my heart." Nodding, smiling, and tapping she went on. "I know it. My family is in my heart."

2003 Seattle

The Personal Village™ Project

The personal village project has the mission to revitalize community in the immediate lives of every person on the planet. It is devoted to encouraging every individual to strengthen the circles of people around him or her, and to encourage others to do the same.

At this time, the Personal Village project, which includes this and other books, seminars, and workshops, is growing. You can become an active member of the project by going right to work nourishing your own personal village and by encouraging those close to you to do the same.

The Web site *www.personalvillage.com* is updated regularly. Check it from time to time to learn about new books, films and resources, additional bibliography, the calendar of events and author appearances. Also on the site you can download copies of the Discussion Guide and the Community Effectiveness Test.

Additional copies of the book may be ordered from the website.

ACKNOWLEDGMENTS

This book has evolved out of the ancients who passed their wisdom forward to this time in history plus the lessons that thousands of people have taught me about community. I owe them all a debt of gratitude for their contribution.

I am particularly thankful to my wife, Peggy, who has stood by me for the 25 years it has taken to write this. Sometimes it felt like I was working on Marv's folly, but her encouragement kept me going. Jean Hirss has also been a steady support from the very beginning to the final proof read. I owe her a deep debt of gratitude. Susan Lamont was my editor who gently and firmly held my hand as this was written. Jennifer McCord stood by as the publishing consultant, always looking several months ahead and keeping me on task. Susan and Jennifer's participation made this book possible. Tami Taylor typeset the book. Her gracious presence and great skill are deeply appreciated. Jennifer Jolly was very helpful with her legal counsel. Jamey Ballot wrote the cover text. Iskra Johnson created the magnificent cover.

Many others have supported the life of this book: Carolyn Attneve, Ceci Miller, Jane Adams, Bonnie Bledsoe, Valerie Sensabaugh, Bob Hermer and Carol Orlock. My readers: Larry Andrews, John Ashford, Ann Stillwater, Jane Nakajima, Pat Mathiesen, Patricia Reutebuch, June Gabriel, Maggie Louden, Oona Gangler, and David Mathiesen all offered suggestions which greatly improved the depth of this work.

Writing this book has been emotionally intense for me. The loving presence of my coterie mates: David York, Marion Evans and Caron Harrang, has been an steadying anchor for which I am deeply grateful.

And finally I want to acknowledge that ultimately I always felt that a force greater than myself was the true author of this book. I was merely the scribe.

COMMUNITY EFFECTIVENESS TEST

Pick a small community cell within which you belong – like a relationship, family, church, prayer group, work team or a board of directors – and rank your degree of fulfillment in each of the following areas:

1. To what degree does this group address your needs for food, shelter and physical safety and comfort?

least   1   2   3   4   5   most

2. Do you feel emotionally safe with these people?

least   1   2   3   4   5   most

3. How strong is your sense of belonging? i.e. do you feel included?

least   1   2   3   4   5   most

4. Are your needs for human warmth, affection and touch, being met in ways which are appropriate for this group?

least   1   2   3   4   5   most

5. Do you have adequate opportunity to be as competent and creative as you are capable within this circle of people?

least   1   2   3   4   5   most

6. To what degree do you feel personally affirmed by the people in this group?

least   1   2   3   4   5   most

7. How much does this group address your need to be involved in a greater meaning which feeds your soul?

least   1   2   3   4   5   most

How To Interpret The Community Effectiveness Test

I called this the Community Effectiveness test because it gives a very easy measure of how well you think this particular community cell is satisfying the basic human needs of every single individual.

I am not going to tell you what this test means. You have the wisdom inside of yourself to analyze the results of this test. Remember this is only how you see this group at this point in time. Others may score this test quite differently. Here are some ways you can proceed:

- After scoring the test sit and contemplate what you have before you. Are you surprised? Does it suggest some area that needs attention? Is there a way you can lend your energy and good heart to bring about improvement? Write down what comes to you and any ideas which spring up in you about how to strengthen this community circle.

- If you have enough mutual trust you could suggest every member of the circle take the test and then sit together and talk about what the results suggest about how to improve the satisfaction of every member.

- If you are stuck, go talk with a friend in that particular circle and see what they think. If you do not feel safe talking with someone in that circle find a trusted person outside who does not have any opinion or vested interest in the particular group and discuss your concern with them.

- If the test shows real trouble – at least in your opinion – you could go talk with a professional about what to do.

- Remember this community circle may be an important dimension in your life. Treat what you think about it and how you act with great respect and kindness.

PERSONAL VILLAGE DISCUSSION GUIDE

ABOUT THIS GUIDE

PERSONAL VILLAGE™ shows how people can restore the humanity to their world by fostering stronger ties with the people in their lives. The questions and discussion topics in this guide will encourage readers to explore the complex issues in this compelling new book.

SUGGESTED TOPICS FOR DISCUSSION:

1. Before you began reading Personal Village what were your ideas about the circles of people that support your life? Where did these ideas come from: books or magazine articles, personal experience or memories?

2. How did your understanding about the personal circles of people around you change as you read this book? Were any of your earlier ideas challenged or confirmed?

3. Marv Thomas draws from many sources—scholarly studies, existing books, historical examples, movies and TV shows, etc.—to give examples of how human interaction leads to the formation of community. Did you find any of these sources particularly useful in reinforcing the notion of Personal Village? Were there any that seemed to contradict it?

4. What are the novel challenges in today's world that you are facing as you move to form more meaningful connections with the people around you?

5. The author suggests that the advertising and media depictions of relationships distort our understanding of human interaction. Has that been your experience, and if so how?

6. Think of and discuss any institutions (church, salon, fellowship, professional organization, etc.) that can help people come together in a positive way. Can you think of any institutions—formal or informal—that might isolate individuals from a positive, supportive community experiences?

7. The author repeatedly mentions the values of his upbringing and how they led to his studies of interpersonal and group dynamics. How has your upbringing influenced your experience of your Personal Village?

8. According to Thomas's sources, "Civilization has changed more in the past half century than at any time in human history." How has the modern world placed individuals at greater risk of isolation and how has it offered greater potential to overcome this isolation? What has been your personal experience of these issues?

9. Do you think that technology abets or inhibits the formation of Personal Villages?

10. Is it your experience that relationships forged in the heat of a crisis are inherently stronger, or have the ones established before the onset of a personal crisis been stronger and more resilient?

11. Do you think that being purposeful and strategic in your relationships undermines your sincerity? If so, can you think of ways to enhance your own Personal Village that are consistent with your values and integrity?

12. How do your think "roaming" and "The Rule of Seven" worked in ancient human evolution? Do you think that primal instincts, like fear of strangers, impacts how you move about in your Personal Village?

13. What are some ways you can seek out a group or organization that best suits your interests and personality? What are some of the indications that an organization's members or group dynamic might be "wrong" for you?

A Conversation With Author
MARV THOMAS

Q. In your book, you refer to the bedrock values of your rural up-bringing. How do the lessons of your formative years play into your concept of the Personal Village™?

A: I grew up in a family that had just migrated off the farm. The values they brought with them included community, though they did not call it that. They simply looked after each other, supported births and stood by at deaths, and observed the rit-ual of family life by gathering often for big dinners, trips to the cemetery and to Sunday church. I simply grew up experiencing the richness of a warm circle of well-known folk and assuming that an extended circle of people would always be available to me. When I left home and moved into a modern, fragmented, hurry-hurry society I was simply shocked at how isolated I felt. My childhood experiences gave me a template about how to have a vital personal community to support my personal life. And I learned that I need to support the same thing for the people around me.

Q. In what ways have people become more distant from one an-other? Aren't the Internet and digital media making us more "connected" than ever?

A: Oh, many influences in the modern world have acted to cause more distance between us. Our mobility is one thing. Instead of wandering around in our natural neighborhoods, we drive miles to meet someone for coffee or spend hours in a commute. Another feature of modern society is our devotion to being in a hurry. We scurry here and there with such speed that we do not take the time to stop and have a leisurely conversation. And when we do slow down we too often are seduced into plastering a phone to our ear or watching the television instead of simply talking in a contact-rich way with the people who are right in front of us.

The electronic ways of communicating have evolved naturally to compensate for our lack of connection. Now we can hurry and talk with someone at the same time, that is if we do not drive into someone in the process. We can say what we want to important people via e-mail and come back later to see how they responded. This is efficient and contributes to our productivity, but it also leads to fragmentation and hurriedness. The digital world is a blessing and curse.

Q. What are some examples of "bad communities," and what can people do to avoid them?

A: Domestic violence makes a family community bad. A bully at school or work makes the school or workplace community bad. A community that is dominated by a control freak is a bad community. A leader who used the community members for their own advantage creates a bad community. A community where the members do not take care of each other is bad.

If the community circle you find yourself in feels wrong in some way, it probably is. What you can do is take the community effectiveness test to orient yourself in a more precise way to what is wrong. Then talk with friends outside of the community. Consult this book for clues about how to bring about changes. If it is possible, talk with other members of the community circle and see if you can collectively agree on a way to bring about positive change. Always think about trying to bring harmony between people and to find a way where everyone's needs are being met to some degree.

Q. Forming a Personal Village demands that you consciously connect with the people that make up your world—neighbors, the people you encounter every day during your commute, the person who serves you coffee at Starbucks, etc. Does this mean that one has to be outgoing and dynamic to have a Personal Village? Are there techniques that "wallflowers" can follow to achieve greater depth to casual relationships?

A: Well, extroverts do have an easier time forming connections. For the rest of us there are lots of ways. The best is to simply hang out with people who are doing things that are interesting to you. If you hang out long enough you will begin to see ways to become involved and the others will naturally begin to include you.

ORDER FORM

Qty.	Title	Price	Can. Price	Total
	Personal Village by Marvin Thomas	$16.95	$22.95	
	Shipping and Handling			
	Add $4.95 in US			
	Sales tax (WA state residents only, add 8.9%			
	Total Enclosed			

Method of Payment:

❑ Visa   ❑ Mastercard   ❑ Check or money order enclosed

— — — — — — — — — — — — — — — — — —   ___/___

Card Number   Exp. Date

_____

Signature

Telephone Orders:
Call 1-800-461-1931
Have your credit card ready.

International Tel. Orders:
Toll free 1-877-250-5500
Have your credit card ready.

Fax Orders:
425-398-1380
Fill out this form and fax.

Postal Orders:
Hara Publishing
P.O. Box 19732
Seattle, WA 98109

Email Orders:
harapub@foxinternet.net

Name:_____
Address:_____
City:_____ State:_____ Zip:_____
Phone: (   )_____ Fax: (   )_____

Quantity discounts are available.
Call 425-398-3679 for more information.
Thank you for your order!